Related Titles

Grammar Source
Math Source
Word Source
Writing Source

Test Prep and Admissions

Caffeine

WILL NOT HELP YOU PASS THAT TEST

Facts, Strategies, and Practical Advice to Help You Succeed in High School

by Cynthia and Drew Johnson

Simon & Schuster

NEW YORK · LONDON · SYDNEY · TORONTO

Kaplan Publishing
Published by SIMON & SCHUSTER
Rockefeller Center
1230 Avenue of the Americas
New York, NY 10020

Contributing Editor: Jon Zeitlin
Editorial Director: Jennifer Farthing
Project Editors: Charli Engelhorn and Anne Kemper
Production Manager: Michael Shevlin
Content Manager: Patrick Kennedy
Interior Page Layout: Renée Mitchell
Cover Design: Mark Weaver

Manufactured in the United States of America
Published simultaneously in Canada

10 9 8 7 6 5 4 3 2 1

October 2005

ISBN-13: 978-0-7432-7966-6
ISBN-10:   0-7432-7966-2

For information regarding special discounts for bulk purchases, please
contact Simon & Schuster Special Sales at 1-800-456-6798 or
business@simonandschuster.com.

TABLE OF CONTENTS

ABOUT THE AUTHORS

Cynthia Johnson is the author of several educational books for young people, two of which received the prestigious Parent's Choice Gold Award in 1995, and were listed in *Curriculum Administrator* magazine's "Top 100" educational products for 1996. **Drew Johnson** is an education writer and editor, creating workbook, textbook, and Web-based education materials for children of all ages. The Johnsons have authored Kaplan's *Ultimate Guides*, *No-Stress Guides*, and *Parent's Guides* to various statewide standardized tests.

ACKNOWLEDGMENTS

Many thanks to the friends, family members, and colleagues whose input helped shape this book, especially Joy Aiken, Margaret Brantley, Melanie Hall, Chris Moran, Tom Pearson, Jimmy Perez, George Saunders, Carl Shepherd, and Vanita Trippe. We would also like to thank our students, past and present, who helped us appreciate the challenges involved in learning to learn. Their struggles and triumphs have been our motivation.

Introduction

The Power of Learning

Caffeine Will Not Help You Pass That Test is not the only study guide available to you. In fact, there are plenty of others to choose from. So why come out with yet another book on learning, you ask? Simple. Most of the books out there don't address the real obstacles that keep you from doing as well as you want to in school. They outline note-taking abbreviation systems, but they don't tell you how to figure out what you should be writing down in the first place. They cover how to format a bibliography, but they don't tell you how to select a paper topic that won't bore you to tears.

Our book is different. We believe that about 95 percent of your success at school depends on motivation, good time management, confidence, and a desire to excel—not on what color highlighting pen you use. The details involved in doing well academically are easy to pick up. It is the fundamentals that are hard to master. And it's the fundamentals that form the primary focus of *Caffeine Will Not Help You Pass That Test*.

IS THIS BOOK FOR YOU?

If you are already an A student and your goal is to graduate with a 4.0 grade point average, you probably do not need this book. You have already mastered the fundamentals and need help only fine-tuning your details. This book will not give you what you need.

If, however, you are . . .

- A high school student struggling to earn at least a B average
- A high school student with erratic grades—A's, F's, and everything in between
- A student with a part-time job and little time to spare
- A student who feels you are not living up to your potential

. . . then *Caffeine Will Not Help You Pass That Test* is the book for you.

OUR APPROACH

GREEN or YELLOW?

Don't sweat the details.

Many books about studying include a lot of quizzes and memorization lists for you. Not this book. Quizzes and lists work very well for many types of skills, but when you are learning to learn more effectively, the main changes you need to make have nothing to do with memorization. What holds most students back is a pattern of behavior—maybe a pattern they are not even aware of—that thwarts their desire to succeed. We point out common bad academic habits, explain the direct and indirect effects of these habits, and offer advice on how to change your ways for the better.

Sure, changing an ingrained behavior pattern is much harder than memorizing a list. It is also a much more effective way to improve your learning skills. That is our main goal: to help you develop the skills you need to learn *anything*, from art history to zoology. We want you to dump the belief that there is some subject out there that you simply can't tackle and discover the pleasures of learning for the sake of learning, the fun of mastering something new, and the thrill of discovering universes full of information you never knew about before.

KAPLAN

BUT AREN'T GRADES IMPORTANT?

You bet they are. We wish the world did not insist on labeling people with numbers and letters that are supposed to show how smart they are, but that's the way it is. Like it or not, teachers, employers, and admissions officers will judge you based on your grades and test scores. Luckily, as we will show you, you have a lot of control over both.

Throughout this book, we offer many tips, techniques, and "tricks" that will help you improve your performance on tests and research papers. We tell you how to maximize your score on essay tests, short-answer tests, and multiple-choice tests. We offer basic advice on how to approach the SAT and other standardized tests. We even give you a plan of attack for taking tests and writing papers when you haven't had time to prepare or study.

WE KNOW THERE'S MORE TO LIFE THAN SCHOOL

You have probably been hearing all your life about how important it is for you to get a good education. Well, it is important. People with more education get better, higher-paying jobs and tend to live longer than people with less education. That is pretty motivating.

But getting a good education does not mean locking yourself in the library until you graduate from high school. In the first place, it would be pretty stupid to spend the prime of your youth locked in a library. In the second place, some of you have jobs and other responsibilities that make locking yourself in the library a practical impossibility. And in the third place, being a good student and a well-rounded person means having some interests and experiences outside of school.

We are not about to tell you to study ten hours a day and give up anything that you find fun. Fun is a necessary part of a happy life. What we will show you is how to come up with a schedule you can live with—one that makes the most of your study time and allows you take part in the activities you enjoy most. It takes a little willpower and some honest soul searching, but it can be done.

IT'S UP TO YOU

We could point out trouble spots and give advice for 100 pages or 1,000, and you could read those pages once or a dozen times, but until you make the commitment to act, nothing will change. But even when you do make the commitment, change does not always come easily. That is why we recommend that you treat building your learning power like you would treat starting a new workout regimen: Start small, and build your way up.

We have organized this book to help you do that. Chapter 1 covers the "bare-bones minimum" requirements of academic success. Chapters 2 through 10 build on those requirements. And chapter 11 is there to act like your coach, offering inspirational thoughts and facts to help get you over the rough spots. The "Plug In" exercises throughout the book provide additional practice as well as insights into your learning style, strengths, and weaknesses.

When you're ready, you can start your learning regimen by turning this page....

Section 1

Don't Miss This

Chapter 1

Bare-Bones Minimum

Before we talk about studying or note taking or paper writing, we need to cover the bare-bones minimum requirements of learning and earning good grades. One, you need to maintain a solid relationship with your teacher, and two, you need to act like a good student. This may surprise you, but being successful in school involves more than just brains and hard work (although brains and hard work are both very important). Doing well has a lot to do with how other people think about you and with how you present yourself. Luckily, mastering the bare-bones minimum is easy, and the payoff is quick. Even if you read nothing else in this book, if you can apply what you learn in this chapter, you will find your performance in school improving almost overnight.

First, we will help you understand what it is your teacher wants from you. Then we will show you how to give your teacher what he wants without having your classmates think you are a dork.

Try This

Before you read this chapter, answer the following questions honestly:

1. Have you missed any class more than three times in the past four months?
2. Have you been late to any class more than three times in the past four months?
3. Have you been reprimanded for disrupting a class or falling asleep during class in the past four months?
4. Have you forgotten to complete an assignment more than once in the past four months?
5. Has your teacher ever caught you cheating or lying?

If you answered "yes" to any of these questions, you are not living up to the minimum standard of behavior expected of good students. Read this chapter carefully.

WHO IS YOUR TEACHER AND WHAT DOES SHE WANT?

To build a good relationship with your instructors, you have to understand where they are coming from—what motivates them, what angers them, what makes them happy. While you are reading this, try to put yourself in an instructor's shoes for just a minute and see things from her point of view.

Who Is Your Teacher?

Your teacher is someone who has spent many years learning, working, and training to help you excel in life. You probably already know this, but high school instructors do not make very much money. They often make less than half of what someone with the same amount of education would earn in another job. So why did they go through all the trouble? Because they really, really want to give you a good education. It's their mission. It's something they believe in and are passionate about.

Unfortunately, a lot of teachers have it rough. Many schools have little money to spend on materials, so teachers can't even get chalk and paper, much less the latest computer software. Some schools have problems with criminal or violent students, which makes teachers feel threatened. Teachers tend to feel that they get all the blame if anything goes wrong in a classroom, but they get no reward or recognition for a job well done. Because of complicated pressures from school boards and administrators, teachers also feel like they have little freedom to try new approaches to teaching and solving problems. The job is so difficult and frustrating, in fact, that many teachers leave the profession within five years.

Ever wish you could sneak into the teachers' lounge or eavesdrop on a conversation between a group of your instructors? Do you wonder what they talk about? Most likely, you would hear them talk about their frustration with rules and requirements that make no sense to them. They might talk about not having the resources they need or the professional freedom they want. And, yes, they do talk about students. They complain about students who show no

KAPLAN

interest in learning. They worry over students who have a lot of potential but no motivation. And then, sometimes, they brag. They brag about students who have made breakthroughs in difficult subjects. They brag about having a good class session in which all the students participated actively. They brag about students who go the extra mile and do exceptional work. They brag because they are proud of their students. It's that pride that makes them want to be teachers. That's what keeps them going.

Note to Self

Here's a commonsense tip that many students overlook: *Know your instructor's name, and know how to spell it correctly.* Turning in a test or paper on which you have misspelled or completely mistaken your teacher's name makes it look like you can't even master basic information. On the first day of class, if your instructor does not write his or her name on the blackboard, raise your hand and ask for the correct spelling and preferred title (Dr., Ms., Mr., etcetera).

What Does Your Teacher Want?

Nothing excites teachers more than the feeling that they are actually helping you learn something. Your learning and achievement are the tests of a teacher's skill, and, of course, your teachers want to feel like they are doing good work. If they had to write out a wish list of the things they want out of their jobs, here's what it would include:

- To see your performance improve over time.
- To make you excited about learning and improving in the future, even after you leave their classes.
- To be treated with respect and honesty.
- To know, at the very least, that all students are trying their best.
- To get a really big raise!

**An apple for the teacher every once in a while is fine,
but cash gifts are not a good idea.**

Okay, so you can't do anything right now about getting your teacher a raise. But you can help fulfill four out of five of these wishes, and that's not bad!

We know this is probably easier said than done. Before we get down to details on how you should interact with your teacher, let's talk about a couple of things that might hold you back: worrying about your image and disliking your teacher.

Note to Self

Follow the syllabus.

Many high school instructors prepare syllabi, or course outlines, for their students. These are often very detailed, and include daily assignments, due dates for papers, test dates, grading policies, and other important information. Make sure you get a copy if one is available! Not only will a syllabus help you plan ahead, it will help you understand what your teacher expects of you. Your teachers put a lot of effort into their course syllabi, so make sure you read them carefully and refer to them often.

BEING TOO COOL CAN TRIP YOU UP

Why is it that the students who show up late, forget their assignments, cut up in class, and act like they don't care about anything seem so cool? And why do students who sit in the front row, raise their hands to answer every question, never miss class, and act all concerned about their grades seem like *such dorks*? If this is the way you feel, you are not alone. Those cool students appeal to us because they seem to be rebelling against authority, and Americans love rebels. Hey, our founding fathers, guys like Benjamin Franklin and Thomas

KAPLAN

Jefferson, were some of the biggest rebels ever, right? Also, as a country, we tend to distrust intellectuals to an almost embarrassing degree. Our heroes are folks like frontiersman Davy Crockett and pilot Amelia Earhart, not super-geniuses like Albert Einstein. We pay millions of dollars to see movies like *Dumb and Dumber*, but would rather have our teeth pulled than watch a Shakespeare play. It's pretty weird when you think about it.

The dog ate my homework!

Benjamin Franklin might have been a rebel but he probably never offered this lame excuse to his teachers.

It's natural that you would rather be seen as cool than as a dork or suck-up. "Coolness" is an attractive concept—especially since cool students obviously do a lot less school work than non-cool students. But prizing your rebel reputation over your education is a mistake. Don't worry, we are not about to urge you to become a complete geek. We will explain in just a little while how you can be a good student without damaging your image. But give the intellectuals of the world a little credit. For example, take a look at Bill Gates, the founder of Microsoft, a giant computer company. Try to imagine him in high school. The word "cool" probably doesn't spring to mind, does it? Today, this guy is very rich and powerful and does not care one bit that you think he looks goofy or that people in high school thought he was a geek.

Unless you are exceptionally lucky, your success in the future will depend completely on your knowledge and your determination. For that reason, it is very important that you take advantage of all the resources available to you in school. Whenever you feel your resolve weakening or feel pressured to downplay your education, try this little trick: Imagine your ten-year class reunion in detail. Think about all the things your education will help you earn: a great job, a nice house, maybe a fancy car. Then think about all those students who goofed off through high school and maybe didn't even get into college. What do you imagine them doing in ten years? Do they still seem cool?

WHEN YOU AND YOUR TEACHER DON'T GET ALONG

Does it seem like your teacher hates you? He cuts you absolutely no slack and never believes a word you say? Or maybe you can't stand him. Maybe he is mean or confusing. Or maybe you just don't like the way he talks or looks or dresses. If any of this sounds familiar, you and your teacher definitely got off on the wrong foot. You probably don't feel like putting forth a special effort for a teacher you don't get along with. Well, get over it. You need to take responsibility for fixing the situation. In order for you to do well and earn better grades, you need to have at least a civil relationship with your teacher. Let's look at some of the things that could have gone wrong, and figure out how to undo the damage.

Maybe You Goofed

Be honest with yourself. Have you been turning in assignments late or not at all? Have you been doing a half-hearted job on your homework? Does your teacher have to tell you to be quiet often? Have you lied to your teacher? If so,

you goofed up. Your teacher probably does not believe you are serious about learning—or worse, she no longer trusts you. She is probably suspicious of you, and not inclined to believe you if a genuine illness or personal problem comes up that interferes with school. This is a tricky problem. It is a lot easier to keep a good reputation than to fix a bad one.

Drooling on your books will not impress your teacher.

The first thing you need to do is finish reading this chapter so you understand the right way to present yourself in class. Make a promise to yourself to do your best to improve your performance. Then, let your teacher know that you understand you made mistakes in the past but that you are going to try hard to live up to her expectations in the future. She may still be suspicious, but if you back up your words with actions, her attitude will change. Remember: Teachers like to see improvement.

Is Your Teacher from Another Planet?

Everyone can tell a story about a freaky teacher. Maybe your ninth-grade government teacher was a five-foot tall bald guy with bad breath and nose hair down to his chin. Maybe your senior English teacher had blue hair, a voice that sounded like a drowning canary, and a single floral dress she seemed to wear every day. Maybe your freshman algebra teacher wore red corduroy knickers, sported a waxed handlebar mustache, and spoke with an unidentifiable foreign accent so thick that the only English word you recognized all semester was *wrong*. These are extreme examples, of course. Sometimes, it's little things that make a teacher seem out of touch, like old-fashioned clothes or silly expressions.

It is easy to tease these teachers and make jokes about them. It's easy, but it's wrong, and it's wrong for many reasons. First, you know the golden rule: Treat people the way you would want to be treated. You probably know very little about your teacher's life and achievements. Don't make all sorts of judgments about a person based on the way she looks or sounds. Second, it is a bad idea to be scornful of your teacher because it makes you less willing to listen to what he has to say. Sure, maybe you wouldn't wish his wardrobe on your worst enemy, but that doesn't mean he doesn't know what he is talking about. Third, few teachers take kindly to students who treat them with a lack of respect. Look at it from a purely practical standpoint. Your teacher gives you your grade. You don't want your teacher to have bad feelings toward you. Be nice.

He's Mean as a Snake

There are some teachers out there who make Marine drill sergeants look like pussy cats. They never smile. Sometimes they yell. And forget about getting them to say something nice about you or your work. What's the sense in even trying to build a good relationship with someone like that?

Most likely, your "mean" teachers act that way because they are trying to motivate you. They are also probably trying to make it clear that they will not tolerate any disruptions in class or silly excuses about homework. These tough teachers can be scary because it seems like they don't like anyone or anything. But believe it or not, just like most teachers, they are impressed by honesty, effort, and improvement. If you do your best for one of these teachers, you may find that you have won a very helpful ally who will advise you and assist you throughout your education. You will also probably find that you learn more from tough teachers than pushovers.

Top Five Reasons for Having a Good Teacher-Student Relationship

1. You will get patience and understanding when you need it most. If you have been honest and respectful to your teacher, he is much more likely to be helpful when a personal emergency or illness interferes with your school work.

2. You will get more out of your classes if you respect your teacher.

3. You will win an ally who can help you with advice about college or graduate school, recommendations for jobs and school applications, and more.

4. You might get academic assistance above and beyond the norm. The more a teacher believes you want to do well, the more she will try to help you.

5. End result: better grades and more brain power.

KAPLAN

Teachers are human. Students are human. Sometimes, two humans just do not like each other. Most of the time, you can figure out what the problem is and address it. But even if you can't, the very least you must do is be polite and respectful toward your teacher. Your teacher owes you the same kind of treatment in return.

PRESENTING YOURSELF WELL

Hopefully, by now you are convinced that getting on your teacher's good side is a smart idea. But how are you supposed to do that? You know that part of developing a good relationship with your teacher is presenting yourself as a good student. But what do good students act like? We have also urged you to "treat your teacher with respect." What does that mean, exactly? Let's take a look at what *not* to do first.

Bad Behavior: Liars, Cut-Ups, and Suck-Ups

You already know that teachers do not like cheaters, liars, bullies, and class clowns. Believe it or not, most teachers also frown on know-it-alls and suck-ups who act like all they care about is making an A. Here are some habits you'll want to avoid.

Liars and Cut-Ups. These guys often skip class or show up late. They interrupt the teacher and make rude comments to classmates. They don't turn in assignments on time but always have some kind of excuse. They read comic books or magazines in class, fall asleep, or write notes to their friends. They disrupt the class just to get a laugh.

Know-it-Alls and Suck-Ups. The suck-ups always seem to be hanging around the teacher's desk. They try to flatter him and bring in cards and presents all the time—and we don't just mean at Christmas time. We're talking Arbor Day, here. Know-it-alls think they are smarter than the teacher. They try to contradict their teachers and feel like they have to comment on everything, even if their comment is irrelevant or unhelpful.

Fundamental Good-Student Guidelines

Acting like a good student doesn't involve you doing anything embarrassing or difficult. You just need to follow these guidelines.

Always come to class. This one simple rule can often boost you up a whole letter grade by itself. The stuff you miss in just one skipped class can really come back to haunt you come test time. Ask any senior, and he'll tell you: No amount of studying afterward can make up for a bunch of missed classes. Another reason you need to show up every day is that it shows the teacher that you are committed to learning something from her class.

Always come on time. It is better to show up late than not at all, but it is still rude and disruptive to walk through a class that has already been in session for several minutes. Your teacher does not think it is cute. Do whatever you have to, but be on time.

Come rested and ready. You are in class on time, but you are a zombie because you stayed up until three in the morning watching TV and you didn't even bring your notebook. Sorry. This is not going to make a good impression. Obviously, sometimes you have to stay up late to finish an assignment (although we will give you tips for avoiding all-nighters in chapter 6), but you should make every effort to get a whole night's sleep on school nights. Be honest—sometimes you stay up really late watching stupid reruns. Cut it out! Go to bed! But before you do, put everything you need to bring to school the next day in your book bag: pen, pencil, notebooks, textbooks, and homework assignments.

Never bring "entertainment" to class. Propping up your textbook so you can read a magazine behind it, write a note, or even finish your homework for another class is not a very original tactic. Plus, it is pretty obvious. Showing up to a lecture armed with the sports section of the newspaper is not likely to go over well either. Even if your instructor doesn't say anything to you about it, you can be sure he notices.

Don't lie or cheat. You know this already. Everybody does. So why do people still lie and cheat? Because they think they can get away with it. Much more often than not, however, liars and cheaters are caught immediately. Your teachers have been around a while and have seen all sorts of tricks pulled. They also have a much easier time spotting plagiarized material than you can possibly imagine. Academic dishonesty can have very serious consequences, where you can be expelled for cheating. What's worse, though, is that there is no faster way to destroy your relationship with your teacher than to lie or cheat. It just isn't worth the risk.

Show common courtesy. Be polite to your teacher and your classmates. You know what we mean. Say "please" and "thanks." Don't call people stupid or laugh at their mistakes. Don't interrupt your classmates or teachers when they are speaking. And when your teacher asks you to do something, do it without grumbling.

Nothing Geeky About It, Right?

You will notice the guidelines above do not mention anything about participating in class, doing homework, or writing papers. We will get to all that later, don't worry. In the meantime, we hope you will agree that sticking to these rules will not make you look like a dork. We hope you also agree that having your teacher trust you and like you is a good idea.

The bare-bones minimum. This is your first step. Commit to putting forward the bare-bones minimum effort, and you will find yourself rewarded with better grades and a better understanding of your subjects.

Section 2

Building Your
Path to Excellence

Chapter 2

Three Skills That Require Little or No Movement

By now, you have made a promise to be in class, awake, with all of the necessary supplies. Before we get into specifics on studying, note taking, and testing, though, we need to cover three important skills: concentrating, listening, and reading. Of course, we know you already know how to read and listen when you feel like it. But let's face it, when a subject is difficult or even boring, it is pretty hard to follow along. This chapter will show you how to strengthen your powers of concentration, then use those powers to listen and read effectively for school.

Try This

Assess your concentration skills now by answering and thinking about the following questions. After practicing some of our techniques, you will notice a big improvement.

1. Do you have a hard time remembering the names of people you just met?
2. Do you often ask people to repeat what they just said?
3. When you are in class, do you ever just "zone out" and lose track of what is going on? For instance, do you ever snap out of a haze and notice your teacher is asking you a question, but you have no clue what she has been saying?
4. When you are reading your textbooks, do you ever find yourself stuck staring blankly at the same page for several minutes?
5. Do you ever finish reading a chapter in your textbook, but feel like you got nothing out of it?

Don't worry! Everyone—even straight-A students—has these problems sometimes.

YOUR MIND NEEDS YOUR BODY

The ancient Greeks had a saying: "A sound mind in a sound body." Actually, they had a lot of sayings, some of them brilliant, some of them downright weird (like "don't urinate while facing the sun"). And, quite frankly, they were more than a little preoccupied with physical beauty. But they were definitely on to something with that whole mind-body connection idea. Your mind can't function at peak efficiency unless your body is healthy and well rested. We are not saying you have to look like an *OC* cast member to be a good student. In fact, the amount of attention the *OC* stars have to pay to their bodies probably leaves them little time for the pursuit of knowledge. But you do need to exercise, get enough sleep, and eat properly. It is more important than you think.

The Stress Cycle

Almost everyone knows what it is like to feel stressed out. Sometimes problems in your personal life, problems at school, problems with your family, or problems with money spring up and just won't go away. You can't sleep, you don't feel like leaving the house, and you start living off potato chips and soda (or some other unhealthy combination). You start to slip up in other areas of your life, maybe showing up late for work or forgetting to do your school assignments. You are tired and worried all the time, and you seem to catch every cough and sniffle that comes your way. Naturally, your grades start to slide. That makes you even more stressed out, causing you to lose more sleep, making you even more tired and forgetful . . . . This is the stress cycle. Not much fun, is it? If you are stressed out, it is no wonder you can't concentrate on your studies.

You can break the cycle by remembering your number one priority: you. One of the fastest ways to short-circuit your stress is by getting some aerobic exercise— just a brisk, 30-minute walk or jog will do—at least four times a week. Medical studies show that people

Does his brain match his biceps?

KAPLAN

who exercise regularly sleep better, get sick less frequently, and feel happier and less stressed about themselves and their lives. Once you start burning off that excess tension, you will find yourself sleepy and calm come bedtime and rested and alert in the morning. Of course, you will need to support your efforts with a well-balanced diet.

We realize that exercising, sleeping, and eating will not actually make some problems go away. Taking care of yourself will, however, give you the mental strength that you need to tackle the important issues in your life. Many students are burdened with multiple responsibilities, and it can be hard to juggle all of them. But no matter what pressures you are facing, remind yourself that you won't be able to satisfy anyone if you are sick, unhappy, and locked in a cycle of stress that makes achievement impossible.

Thin Thighs, Starved Brain

Most likely, someone you know eats less than her body needs because she is determined to look like a supermodel. Maybe that person is you. You wouldn't be alone. It is estimated that one in ten women has an eating disorder of some sort, caused by an overwhelming, unreasonable fear of fat. We are not doctors, and there is probably little we could say about eating and a healthy body image that you haven't already heard, but we will add a few facts to the mountain of arguments against eating improperly.

Even just skipping a couple of meals can make your blood-sugar levels plummet, leaving you dizzy and nauseated. A low-calorie diet (one that gives you fewer than 1,200 calories a day) will make you headachy and irritable within a week or two. Unless you follow a very carefully balanced vegetarian regimen, eliminating meat from your diet can bring on anemia, which makes you feel weak and short of breath, may make you feel cold all the time, and can cause memory problems. Clearly, crash dieting and fasting—even if you do it only every once in a while—will not help you develop the powers of concentration you need to do well in school. Reevaluate your priorities. Would you rather be weak, ignorant, and skinny, or educated, energetic, and healthy?

Mind Boost

Pyramid Power

For online tips on weight, diet, and exercise, including an explanation of the Food Pyramid, visit the Food and Nutrition Information Center site at www.nalusda.gov/fnic/index.html

LIVE IN THE MOMENT

A little while ago, we borrowed a phrase from the ancient Greeks. Now we want to borrow a concept from those modern-day philosophers, the hippies of the 1960s. They advised people to live in the moment, to "be here now." What they meant is that to get the most out of life, we should all stop worrying about the past or future, and live as much as possible in the present, seizing every moment of our lives as they happen. Seizing the day and living in the moment may seem fine when that day is spent at the beach, you may argue, but what about days spent waiting in line at the Department of Motor Vehicles? Granted, some things do not lend themselves to seizing. But if you can apply the idea of living in the moment to your studies, you will greatly increase the amount of time you can spend seizing moments at the beach (or wherever you feel most present in the present).

Concentrate on the present, man!

Here is what we mean: Instead of being bored and kind of irritated that you have to sit through your chemistry class, make an effort to be there—all there—in mind and spirit. Most likely, your classes are only 50 minutes to an hour long. Devote yourself to each class, and nothing else, for those 50 or 60 minutes. Don't look at the clock. Don't think about what you would like for dinner or what you want to do this weekend. Hang on to every word your instructor says as if she were explaining the most fascinating thing in the world. Sure, this might require a leap of the imagination on your part sometimes, but give it a try. Here is what will happen: Time will pass quickly.

KAPLAN

You will remember most of that day's lesson. And because you remember it, you will not have to spend many study hours later trying to learn what you missed when you were busy being bored and irritated.

You have to be in class anyway, so make the most of it. And when we say "make the most of it," we don't just mean "tough it out." We mean squeeze as much out of those classroom hours as you can. Maybe you would rather be watching television or hanging out with your friends, but you can't do those things while you are in school. So instead of wasting time wishing you were doing those things, learn absolutely everything you can while you are in the classroom. Every thing you learn in school is one less thing you have to learn later, at home on a weekend, when you could be relaxing and enjoying yourself.

HOW TO CONCENTRATE

Half the battle in learning to concentrate is deciding that something is important enough to concentrate on. Another big part is being awake and alert enough to pay attention. We have just given you some guidelines on how to stay sharp and some good reasons for focusing your attention on your instructor. But sometimes, even with the best intentions, students become distracted. Some of these tips might help you regain your focus if you find your mind wandering.

Sit up front (away from the window). It can be pretty hard not to watch what your classmates are doing during class or to ignore what you see going on outside. If only wearing blinders were a practical solution. If you find yourself easily distracted, try to sit in the front row of the class. If your seating is assigned, explain to your instructor that you want to be sure to concentrate on the lectures and that sitting up front will help you. You will be less tempted to observe your classmates if you have to turn all the way around to do so.

Calm a jumpy brain. Are you an energetic person whose mind races with thoughts and ideas? If so, you are probably very creative but have trouble concentrating for long periods of time. There are a couple of things you can do to help yourself focus. First, if you have enough time in between classes, try to get outside and walk briskly for five or ten minutes around the block or around the outside of the school building. While you are walking, do not think about school or anything important. Just take good, deep breaths and try to let go of any tension.

Another trick you might try is meditation. You don't have to twist your legs up like a pretzel or chant anything. Just try to find a comfortable spot where you can sit for five minutes. It helps if you can find a quiet place, but that might be hard in the middle of a school day, so just do your best to find a spot where you will be left alone. Close your eyes, sit up straight, and let your arms and legs relax. Picture something simple, still, and peaceful in your mind: a lighted candle, a tree, a full moon, or anything you find calming. Try to focus your mind on that image while breathing deeply and slowly. Do this for about five minutes.

Both of these techniques will help "reset" your mind and get you ready to concentrate on school.

Limit your caffeine and sugar intake. No doubt about it, an ice cold soda and a chocolate bar make an appealing snack. If you indulge yourself only every once in a while, then you have nothing to worry about. But if your caffeine habit entails three or more Cokes or coffees a day and hardly an afternoon goes by without a sugar fix, you need to cut back, and not just because of your dental health. Too much caffeine, as you know, can make you jumpy, which, in turn, makes it hard to concentrate. Too much sugar can have you bouncing off the walls one hour then feeling listless the next as your blood sugar crashes. Both of these effects ruin your ability to concentrate.

HOW TO LISTEN

We have already covered how you can make sure you are in the right frame of mind and ready to concentrate in class. But once your instructor starts talking, any number of factors can make it hard to follow along. The main problems students tend to have are:

- Your instructor speaks too quickly for you and covers a lot a material in each class. This leaves you bewildered, barely grabbing on to one idea before the next one comes up.

- Your instructor seems to speak much more slowly than you can think. (Actually, most people can think much more quickly than they, or their teachers, can speak.) Because of this, your mind wanders and gets off track.

KAPLAN

- You simply have no idea what the instructor is talking about. He uses words and phrases that are completely unfamiliar to you, and you feel like the whole lesson is over your head.

Let's go over these problems one at a time and learn how to deal with them. In chapters three and four, we will go into more detail on how you can figure out what your teacher wants you to remember and take notes accordingly. First, you have to learn to follow along.

Too Much, Too Fast

Some teachers set very ambitious goals and fill each lesson with tons of information. They often lecture continuously, rarely stopping to ask questions or answer them, and write a lot of material on the blackboard. That can leave you feeling left in the dust. There are several things you can do to make the lessons more accessible to you.

Sneak a peek at the lesson ahead of time. Skim through any parts of your textbook your teacher will be covering before class. This gives you an orientation to the material and a sense of where your instructor is heading in a lecture. That way, even if you lose track of what she is saying, you have a chance of getting back in sync later. Look further on in this chapter for some more information on skimming or previewing.

Raise your hand. If your teacher moves on from one topic to another before you think you understand it, raise your hand and ask for clarification. You must be considerate of your teacher and your classmates when you do this. If you don't understand something because you didn't do the assigned homework or reading, it is not fair for you to slow down the whole class and ask the teacher to explain something you should have already familiarized yourself with. If you have made every effort to stay caught up, though, then by all means ask your question. You will be doing the class a favor.

Be as specific as possible. Do not complain vaguely, "I don't get it." Try to rephrase what your teacher said in your own words and point out exactly what you don't understand. For example, instead of saying to your history instructor, "Could you tell me again what you mean by *gerrymandering*?", you might say, "Sometimes whatever political party is in power reconfigures voting districts in weird ways, which is called *gerrymandering*. But what good does that do them?"

Rephrasing what you instructor says gives him a chance to correct any misunderstanding you might have. Asking a specific question helps the instructor figure out exactly where you got off track, which makes it easier for him to clear up your confusion.

Too Slow

Next week's math test. Your dress for the formal. A gift for your brother's birthday. Bearded French fries doing a tango on a grill full of hamburgers while singing "Disco Inferno." Quite a few important, unimportant, and bizarre thoughts can flash through you mind in the time it takes for your teacher to move from his desk to the overhead projector. One minute you are following along carefully, then some pause in the class or some boring part of the lesson comes along and your brain floats off to a tropical island.

If this is a problem you face often, reread the section above on concentration. You must decide that listening and concentrating are important, and promise yourself that you will try as hard as you can to focus. Here are some other ideas to help you anchored.

Rephrase, repeat, and apply. Use slow parts of the class to review material in your head. Go over concepts and definitions that your instructor has introduced and try rephrasing them in your own words. Then repeat your new phrases and definitions to yourself and try to memorize them. You might also try applying your new definition to examples. For instance, your English instructor might have just explained that "iambic pentameter refers to a line of verse containing five feet, or poetic units, in which the first syllable is unstressed and the second syllable is stressed." You rephrase this in your head as something like "iambic pentameter goes da-DUM da-DUM da-DUM da-DUM da-DUM." Or you might come up with examples, like "Around the rock the rugged rascal ran."

Good learning requires a good foundation.

Test your psychic abilities. Try to figure out what your instructor's next move will be. What will he cover next? What kinds of examples will he use? How might this material appear on the next exam? This not only keeps you involved in the class, it trains you to follow your instructor's thought process, which will help you to do better on assignments.

Over Your Head?

Are you just plain lost? This is a common feeling, especially for students entering their first year of high school. You might be introduced to teaching styles and study demands you have never encountered before. The work might be much tougher than anything you have been asked to do in the past. You might not have the background that other students in the class have. Don't panic! None of these is reason to give up. You just need to get yourself up to speed as quickly as possible. Good note taking, studying, and test-taking skills will all help, and we will cover all of those areas soon. Listening carefully, even when you don't understand everything clearly, is another important skill, and that is what we are going to talk about right now.

The feeling of being lost comes from not having a sufficient foundation of knowledge in a certain area. Each teacher you learn from assumes you have mastered a certain set of skills. Your kindergarten teacher assumed you could speak and understand English. Your algebra teacher assumed you could multiply and divide. Your American history instructor assumes you understand how the U.S. government works and are familiar with the basic timeline of our country's history. Each teacher tries to build on an earlier foundation. The trouble is that sometimes, for whatever reason, students lack pieces of their foundations. When a new instructor comes along and tries to build, the new "bricks" of knowledge have nothing to rest on. They just topple over.

Mind Boost

Here are just a few examples of some useful movies:

Literary Movies

The Crucible (1996)

Henry V (1945 or 1989)

The Last of the Mohicans (1992)

Romeo and Juliet (1968 or 1996)

Sense and Sensibility (1995)

Historical Movies

Gandhi (1982)—twentieth-century India

A Man for All Seasons (1966)—England in the 1500s

Patton (1970)—World War II

Schindler's List (1993) —World War II

Movies about Science

A Brief History of Time (1992)—Stephen Hawking's theories

Apollo 13 (1993)—rocket science

That is basically what is happening when you feel like a class is over your head. Bricks are just toppling over because there is no structure in place to keep them together. So how are you supposed to concentrate and listen carefully?

Sometimes it helps to go to the movies. In subjects like history and literature, you can sometimes build up pieces of your foundation by watching good, reputable films. Many highly regarded film versions of plays, books, and historical events are available at your video store or library—but be careful! Some movies are based on real people, but they play fast and loose with the facts. Some film versions of famous books do not stick very close to the original plot line. Still, there are many fine, exciting, accurate films and documentaries available that can help get you up to speed. Ask your teacher or your local librarian for advice.

Often, instructors in other subjects, even science and math, can recommend films to help you. These are not always available in regular video rental stores, but your teacher can steer you in the right direction.

Write it down and move on. If your instructor uses a word or phrase in class that you don't understand, do not freeze up or zone out. Write the words down, and keep focusing on the lecture as best you can. Most likely, you will be able to get something out of a lecture, even if you do not understand all of it. As soon as possible after class, look up the word that confused you in the index of your textbooks or the dictionary. If you can't find it, go ask your teacher for clarification.

Accept the fact that you might have to work twice as hard as other students. Don't give up on a class just because it is hard. What if you gave up on learning to walk just because you fell down a lot at first? You have probably learned to do a lot of difficult things in your life, like doing a front handspring or making three-point shots in basketball or playing a difficult piano piece without a mistake. After you succeeded, you probably felt proud of yourself, and rightly so. You can get the same pride out of mastering a difficult subject at school.

Remember, unless you put in the time and energy to do the "foundation repair" you need in a certain subject, you will never be able excel in that area. Give yourself a chance to succeed. You may find out you have talents you did not even know about.

HOW TO READ

Reading a textbook is not like reading a magazine, a newspaper, or a book you are reading for fun. The material is much denser and often much drier. You will not get much out of your textbook if you read it casually or carelessly. In fact, you probably will not get much out of a chapter in your textbook if you read it just once. To master what you are reading, you need to go over it three times.

Stop groaning! It isn't as bad as it sounds. The reading method we favor is called by many names and used by many instructors. We call it the "3 S" method: Skim, Scrutinize, and Sweep Up. If you follow this method, you will probably find yourself spending more time with your textbook than you used to. You will also find that studying for tests will become a whole lot easier.

> ### Did You Know...
>
> *It was the best of study times, it was the worst of study times . . . .*
>
> In a recent online survey, we asked when people studied most effectively, and how they managed to stay alert while studying. Here are the results from over 1,550 respondents.
>
> Best Study Time
>
> | | |
> |---|---|
> | 41% | Evening |
> | 30% | Morning |
> | 16% | Witching hour |
> | 12% | Afternoon |
>
> Preferred Awakeness Aid
>
> | | |
> |---|---|
> | 47% | Caffeine |
> | 26% | Exercise |
> | 8% | Sugar |
> | 8% | Cold shower |
> | 3% | Eyelid tape |
> | 2% | Electroshock |
> | 1% | Nonprescription drugs |
> | 1% | Prescription drugs |
> | 1% | Herbal remedies |

Skim

This is the first reading phase, often called "previewing." Before your instructor covers a certain chapter and before you sit down to read it carefully, skim through your assigned reading. Look at the pictures and illustrations and read the captions underneath. Read the introductory paragraph and all the headings in the chapter. If there is a summary or quiz at the end of the chapter, read it, too. Flip to the table of contents and see how this chapter fits in context with the rest of the book.

Skimming ahead of time not only helps you understand your teacher's lessons better, it helps lay the groundwork for careful, concentrated reading, which is your next step.

Note to Self

What does the format mean?

Before you start reading a chapter in your textbook, read the table of contents and the introduction, then flip through twenty or thirty pages. Notice the way any color, shading, or boldface type is used. Are there headings that run across the tops of the pages? Are summaries given at the end of chapters? Your textbook authors and designers included all of these elements to make your book easier to use. They highlight certain material by setting it off in certain ways. Rules and formulas may be set off in shaded boxes, while new terminology may be printed in bold. If you can figure out what pattern your textbook follows, your skimming and scrutinizing will both be easier.

Scrutinize

After you have skimmed, you need to set aside time to scrutinize your assigned reading. How much time you set aside depends on your reading style and your personal preferences. Answer the questions below to figure out what is best for you.

Try This

With 1 being "best" and 5 being "worst," rate the following times of day in terms of how much "brain power" you think you have: early morning, late morning, afternoon, evening, night.

Test yourself: Find a watch or clock, and pick up your most difficult textbook. Start carefully reading a chapter you have not gone over before. How many pages can you read before your mind starts to wander?

KAPLAN

Pick your peak time for scrutinizing. You don't always have the luxury of picking the very best time of day in which to read carefully. You can, however, try to schedule your reading for better times instead of worse. Scrutinizing takes a lot of concentration, so you want to be at your sharpest.

Read manageable chunks. You can wear yourself out trying to read 80 pages of a complicated textbook without a break. You will also forget much of what you read. Read only as much as you can concentrate on—but at least ten pages—then take a five-minute break before moving on.

Banish all distractions. As much as you might want to, you can't read carefully in front of the television or in a room where many people are talking. Find a quiet, private place to study. If music helps relax you, great, but make sure you are not paying more attention to the lyrics than your reading. For especially difficult reading, it sometimes help to sit at a table or desk in a comfortable, but straight-backed chair. Curling up on the couch or in bed can be a little too relaxing.

If you can, mark your textbooks. If you own your textbooks, a good technique to help you prepare for the "Sweep Up" reading phase is marking important concepts with a pen or pencil and making marginal notes. Develop a system for marking ideas. For example, you might circle new terminology, put boxes around the names of important people, and underline key concepts and definitions. Do not mark too much! Your marks are meant to guide you in your review of the chapter later. If your pages are covered in lines and circles, you will not know what to focus on. Only mark the essential ideas.

Read critically and ask yourself questions. Question what you read. Pretend you are having a dialog with the person (or people) who wrote your textbook. Evaluate the information you are receiving, and make a note of any blank spots in your understanding or any desire you have for more information. Write your questions in the margin of your textbook or in a notebook. Your instructor may clear up some of your confusion during her lecture. If not, feel free to ask your questions in class.

Biology Review

CAN HERBIVORES DIGEST MEAT?

Herbivores consume only plants or plant foods. Due to the toughness of cellulose-containing plant tissues, herbivores possess ingestive structures for crushing and grinding these tissues and for extracting plant fluids. Their long digestive tracts offer more surface area and time for digestion. Much of the food they consume is indigestible; thus symbiotic bacteria capable of digesting cellulose cohabit the digestive tracts of herbivores. Thus, many herbivores, such as cows and horses, have hooves instead of toes to enable faster movement on the grasslands. They have incisors adapted for cutting and molars adapted for grinding their food. Examples of herbivores include cows, deer, rabbits, horses, zebras, and beavers. Insects or other invertebrates can also be herbivores.

ARE HUMAN VEGETARIANS HERBIVORES OR OMNIVORES?

Carnivores, meanwhile, eat other animals exclusively. In general, carnivores possess pointed teeth and fanglike canine teeth for tearing flesh. They have relatively short digestive tracts due to the easy digestibility of meat. *Omnivores*, on the other hand, are animals that eat both plants and animals. Their digestive tracts enable them to digest and absorb both plant matter and meat.

Interspecific Interactions

A community is not simply a collection of different species living within the same area. It is an integrated system of species that are dependent upon one another to one extent or another. The major types of interspecific interactions are discussed below.

Symbiosis

Symbionts live together in an intimate, often permanent association that may or may not be beneficial to them. Some symbiotic relationships are obligatory—that is, one or both organisms cannot survive without the other. Types of symbiotic relationships are generally classified according to the benefits the symbionts receive. Symbiotic relationships include commensalism, mutualism, and parasitism.

Commensalism. In this relationship, one organism is benefited by the association and the other is not affected (this is symbolized as +/0). The host neither discourages nor fosters the relationship. The remora (shark-sucker), for example, attaches itself by a hold-fast device to the underside of a shark. Through this association, the remora obtains the food the shark discards, wide geographic dispersal, and protection from enemies. The shark is totally indifferent to the association. A similar association links the barnacle and the whale. The barnacle is a sessile crustacean that attaches to the whale and obtains wider feeding opportunities through its host's migrations.

Mutualism. This is a symbiotic relationship from which both organisms derive some benefit. In the instance of the tick bird and rhinoceros, the rhinoceros aids the bird through the provision of food in the form of parasites

Don't Mix These Up on Test Day

These types of symbiosis come up frequently on the SAT II: Biology test:

types of symbiosis

- *Commensalism* is a +/0 relationship in which one organism benefits and the other is unaffected.

- *Mutualism* is a +/+ relationship in which both organisms benefit.

- *Parasitism* is a +/− relationship in which one organism benefits and the other is harmed.

Sample Marked-Up Textbook Page

Sweep Up

Think of this reading as tidying up your understanding. After skimming, scrutinizing, and listening to your instructor's lesson, quickly read through the assigned chapter or chapters again, looking for any messy or confusing areas. Carefully read through any parts you feel weak in.

If, even after Sweep Up, you feel confused, don't just forget about it. Make sure you have mastered the material. You have your foundation to think about, remember? Ask a classmate for some clarification or go to your teacher for extra help.

Speaking of teachers, they can be as difficult to understand as textbooks, can't they? Check out chapter three for the keys to unlocking your teacher's hidden meanings.

Chapter 3

Deciphering Your Teacher

What does your teacher expect from you on test day? Does she think you should have memorized a set of facts and figures? Will she ask you to apply general concepts to specific problems? Will she ask you to write an essay explaining or interpreting something in your own words?

Before you can take notes or study effectively, you need to figure out what kinds of knowledge and skills your instructor expects from you. The easiest way to figure out what your instructor is expecting is to take a look at one of his tests and see how it is put together. Later in this chapter, we will show you how to analyze a test and use it as the basis for your study plan in a course. Unfortunately, you can't wait until after the first test to start taking notes and studying. With that in mind, let's start by going over some tactics you can use to anticipate your instructor's expectations early in the semester.

THREE TYPES OF LEARNING: MEMORIZATION, APPLICATION, AND INTERPRETATION

Most courses you take in high school demand one or more of three types of learning: *memorization*, *application*, and *interpretation*. You might think of these styles along a continuum: Early in your study of a certain discipline, you need to master the basics, which means memorizing many terms and facts. For example, when you first started learning math, you learned to count. You later learned what the terms *addition*, *subtraction*, *odd*, and *even* meant. After you had these ideas down pat, you were asked to apply your new knowledge to math problems—like "show me you understand addition and the idea of '3' and '7' by telling me what 3 + 7 is." This process of memorization and application continued. By now you probably know how to do pretty complex

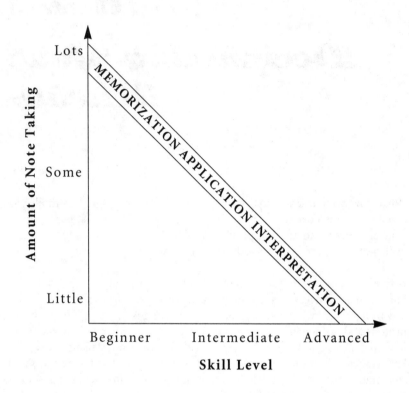

M-A-I CHART

word problems involving algebraic principles. Once the "word" or "real life" problems become very complex, however, you move beyond just applying what you have learned. For example, when astronomers make conclusions about the existence of black holes in space, they use their math and physics skills to interpret what they observe through their telescopes.

All learning relies to some degree on memorization, but memorization alone is often not enough to satisfy your instructor. The trick is to figure out when memorization is enough, when application is expected, and when interpretation will be demanded. Check out the quick "Try This" to see how well you "read" your teacher.

Try This

Decide whether memorization, application, or interpretation will be called for on a test of the subject matter below.

1. In your Intro to Art History class, you are shown many slides of paintings and given the names of the artists and the date each painting was created.
2. You have been learning about sines, cosines, and tangents in your trigonometry class.
3. You and a lab partner have been conducting an independent experiment on the eating habits of mice.
4. Your English teacher has just covered the rules for using semicolons.
5. In your 20th Century American Poetry class, you have been reading a lot of poems by Robert Frost.

All of these types of learning are very important, and each has its place. Usually, one kind is stressed more than the others in any given course, but even in the most advanced courses, some memorization is required. Here are some ways to recognize which type of learning your teacher expects of you, both in the course as a whole and within each class period.

Memorization

- Any course called Introduction to . . . or Basic . . . is likely to demand a lot of memorization.
- If your instructor writes phrases, dates, or diagrams on the board, you will probably be responsible for them. This is especially true if your instructor writes out an entire definition, or if the instructor has prepared a slide or overhead sheet ahead of time with dates and definitions on it.
- If your instructor stops and repeats a certain concept or sentence, he is trying to stress its importance. You might be asked to memorize it.
- If your instructor speaks very slowly and deliberately—more so than usual—he is probably trying to give you time to write down what he is saying so you can memorize it.

Application

- Does your instructor ask you to turn in a lot of written homework? She is probably trying to give you practice in applying new skills. You will see more of the same on your test.

- If your instructor spends a lot of class time working through example problems or cases, you will be asked to do something similar on your test.

- Does your instructor put students on the spot, asking them to solve problems on the blackboard or in their heads? That's more application practice.

Interpretation

- Does the class consist mainly of discussion in which the instructor asks a lot of general questions and offers guidance, but the students do most of the talking? If so, your tests will probably demand interpretive skills.

- If your homework consists mainly of reading or observing, your test will focus on interpretation.

- Most literature courses, by nature, demand interpretative skills. So do advanced laboratory science classes and art, film, and music appreciation classes.

Mind Boost

Coming Attractions

Not clear on what "interpretation" entails? Afraid it has something to do with the dreaded "essay question"? Don't worry. In chapter seven, we will help you tackle essay questions and hone your interpretative skills. In chapter nine, you will learn how to write an interpretative paper.

Designing Your Decoding Strategy

Step One: The first thing you need to do when starting off in any class is figure out which type of learning will be stressed throughout the semester or year. This determines what kind of note-taking and class participation strategy you should use (which we will cover in the next chapter). You can use some of the tips above to figure that out. Your syllabus, if you have one, will also give you some clues. It is also a good

KAPLAN

idea to try to find people who have already taken the class you are taking with the same instructor. Ask them what kinds of questions were asked on tests, and what kinds of demands the teacher made.

Step Two: During each class, be on the lookout for shifts in teaching style. Remember, even if your class focuses on interpretation, you could be asked to memorize. The reverse is also true. For example, if a teacher stops an interpretative class discussion and gets up and writes some names and dates on the blackboard, you might have to memorize what she is writing. Or if you teacher stops lecturing and starts asking students to offer their thoughts and opinions on a topic, you may later be asked to offer your interpretation on a test.

Step Three: Have you ever seen one of those Westerns in which some gambler winds up winning everybody's money in an all-night poker game? How could anyone be that lucky, you may have wondered? Actually, winning at cards has more to do with powers of observation than luck. Good gamblers notice things—like how one player scratches his head when he's bluffing and another drums her fingers when she has a good hand. Good students need to use their powers of observation to decode their teachers' gestures and speech. Sometimes it's very easy—especially when there is no "code" to decode. You teacher might simply say, "Now this is very important. . . ." or, "Pay attention." These are obvious sign he wants you to remember what he is saying. Sometimes the clues are harder to pick up on. You teacher may tap her hand or pen on her desk when emphasizing something or repeat a phrase several times. Look for patterns in your teacher's speech and gestures, and try to figure out what the patterns mean.

AFTER THE FIRST TEST

Once you get your first test back, you can stop trying to read your instructor's mind all the time. You have an example, in black and white, of what you instructor expects and what he thinks of your performance. Try not to worry too much if you did not do as well as you hoped. Your graded test is the key to success in the rest of the class.

What Does the Structure Tell You?

Despite your best guesses, teachers can surprise you. For example, in your British literature class you might have expected an essay test that asked for your interpretation of certain poems and stories, but instead you got a fill-in-the-blank test that just asked you to identify the authors and titles of certain passages. Maybe you expected to be tested on how well you memorized some terminology in your psychology class, but instead you were asked to apply the definitions you memorized to certain test cases. Of course, the fact that one test stresses memorization is not a 100-percent guarantee that later tests won't stress application or interpretation, but instructors do tend to stick close to the same format for most of their tests. Based on the kind of test your teacher favors, you can reevaluate your approach to the class and the balance you have struck between memorization, application, and interpretation.

If the test was in short-answer or fill-in-the-blank format . . . Your instructor is probably expecting you to memorize material from class and your textbooks. You will need to take careful notes (see chapter four) and spend study time quizzing yourself (see chapter six).

If the test was a set of problems or cases . . . Application is being stressed here. Math tests are usually application tests, but grammar tests are often application tests, too. When application is the focus, practice is the key.

If the test was in essay or long-answer form . . . You are being asked to interpret something. A mastery of some facts and figures will be

KAPLAN

important in most essay responses, but what your teacher really wants to see is whether you have "digested" the material and made it your own. You will need to explain and defend your own viewpoint on an issue.

What Was the Degree of Depth, Detail, and Difficulty?

Sometimes students can successfully predict the type of test they will face but completely miss the mark on depth, detail, and difficulty. Say you are prepared for a fill-in-the-blank test in literature, and you have written down and memorized all the publication dates and author names your teacher wrote on the board. On test day, however, you discover than he wanted you to know not only all the dates and names from the board, but all the dates and names he mentioned in class along with all the dates and names from the textbook. Or maybe for your biology test you learned the different parts of the human circulatory system but were unable to answer the test question that asks you to explain how the parts work together. Or it could be that your calculus test was just so hard you were blown away. These problems all stem from misjudgments of the level of skill your teacher requires.

Do we have to know this for the test?

Don't ask this question. It makes your teachers think you're lazy.

It can be hard to avoid problems of depth, detail, and difficulty on a first test because you don't know for sure what to expect. Our best advice is to ask former students of that instructor about past tests and prepare for the most difficult questions you think your instructor could ask. On test day, you may find out you learned much more than your teacher expected, and the test may seem easy. Great! After the first test, you will have a good grade, a solid foundation in the course, and a much clearer idea of what kind of performance your teacher expects from you. Studying "too much" is much better than studying too little.

What Can You Learn from Your Teacher's Comments?

Many instructors don't write detailed comments on student tests, but if yours does, count yourself lucky. You can learn a lot about what you are doing wrong and right by paying careful attention to the notes and pointers your teacher makes on your papers. When you see your test paper coming toward you covered with red ink, don't crumple it up in disgust. Wait a day or two, especially if you feel upset or disappointed in your grade, then review your test calmly.

We all find it unpleasant to have our shortcomings pointed out to us, especially if they are pointed out bluntly in writing. Remember, your instructor is not trying to hurt your feelings. He is trying to help you do a better job. He could have just slapped a grade on your test and left it at that, but he took the time to point out weak and strong areas in your work. If there are comments on your test, read them without anger and see if you can learn anything from them that will help you as you continue in the class.

TALK TO YOUR TEACHER

We have talked a lot about "decoding" your instructor, and offered various pieces of advice for understanding what your teacher wants from you. All of the techniques we have covered are useful and important. But if you have tried everything and you still feel like you have no idea what you teacher wants from you, there is one more method you can use to find out: Talk to her.

This technique doesn't work well for all types of questions. You will not be able to get your teacher to tell you what is going to be on your test, for example. Your teacher will also not respond usefully to vague questions, like "What do you expect from me?" or "What do I have to do to make a good grade in this class?" The best way to get something productive out of a student-teacher talk is to have a concrete and specific issue to discuss. Your first test makes an ideal subject.

Mind Boost

File It Away

Don't throw your test away! It is a valuable study tool. Keep it someplace where you won't lose it. In chapter six, we will explain how you can use that test as a road map to success on the next exam.

KAPLAN

If, after going over your first test, you still don't feel like you have a clear idea of what material and skills you are supposed to be mastering, make an appointment with your teacher. Here are some do's and don'ts for your meeting:

- **Don't** just march up to your teacher's desk after she hands back your paper and insist on talking about it right then and there. It is important to set up an appointment so she can block out time just for you and not be distracted by her other responsibilities.

- **Don't** approach your meeting as some kind of argument. If you are upset about your grade, make your appointment for a few days or even a week after you get your test back so you can cool down and evaluate your performance calmly.

If you're not sure what you're supposed to be learning, talk to your teacher.

- **Don't** be late. It is even more important to show up on time for a conference with your teacher than it is to show up on time for class. She is setting aside extra time for you, and it won't look good it you blow it off or keep her waiting.

- **Do** prepare in advance some specific questions about your test that you want cleared up. If you don't understand what you did wrong on a particular question, for example, you should ask. If you don't understand your teacher's comments, ask for clarification.

- **Do** ask for advice on improving in specific weak areas, especially areas your teacher has pointed out to you. If your writing teacher says that your grammar is weak, for example, ask her what you can do to improve it.

Setting up a conference with your instructor is one of the best ways for you to get to know and understand her better and demonstrate your commitment to improving your performance. Even if you are satisfied that you know what you are doing, it is a good idea to meet briefly with each of your instructors at least once so you can find out for sure whether you are on the right track.

Chapter 4
Take Note!

TO NOTE OR NOT TO NOTE

When should you write something down, and when should you ignore it? Wait, don't answer yet—this is a trick question. Actually, you should never ignore what your teacher is saying (unless he's complaining endlessly about some ex-girlfriend or the line at the post office or something unrelated to class). You are awake, alert, and attentive, right? If you are listening carefully, even if you do not write everything down, your brain will register and retain a lot of what your teacher says. You should take notes only when something is noteworthy.

Your new combination of concentration, listening, and teacher-decoding talents should help you identify noteworthy material easily. But as with any skill, practice makes perfect. Give yourself some time to get into a note-taking rhythm and get used to your teacher's lecture style.

HOW MANY NOTES ARE ENOUGH?

Take a look around your typical class and you will see a wide variety of note-taking behaviors. Some students seem to never look up from the notebook on which they are furiously scribbling page after page of detailed notes. Some students write down the date and maybe a doodle. Most fall in between somewhere. Is the doodler a slacker who is sure to fail . . . or someone who knows the material so well already he doesn't need to write anything down? Is the scribbler the obvious A student . . . or a panic-stricken novice who takes way too many notes? The answers are unclear. Both could actually be taking the appropriate amount of notes for them. Exactly what constitutes an "appropriate amount" has mainly to do with your own confidence and your instructor's teaching style, as we'll explain below.

When Is It Noteworthy?

- When your teacher seems to be emphasizing something, or it seems likely that you will be asked to memorize it. (See chapter three for tips on how to pick up on your teacher's signals.)

- When it's a key concept, formula, or definition you think you will be asked to use often or on which other concepts, formulas, or definitions rely (for example, you have to know what the literary term *meter* means before you can learn about different poetic structures.)

- If your teacher writes it down or puts up a slide with writing on it. (Exceptions: If your teacher seems to write almost everything she says on the board or scribbles words down randomly, you don't have to write it all down.)

- If your teacher is giving you important administrative information, like when your next test will be, what the format of the test will be, etcetera.

- If you hear something interesting, weird, funny, or surprising.

- If your hear a word or phrase you don't understand. Don't let hearing unfamiliar words derail your concentration. Write them down and clear up your confusion after class (see below for more note-taking "techniques").

How to Tell Too Much from Too Little

Your notes need to be accurate and useful. Their only purpose is to refresh your memory on important points. Ideally, years from now they will still be helpful and instructive to you. At the very least, your notes need to be able to refresh your memory throughout the semester or term.

Let them eat cake?

If your notes are too sparse, you might be left wondering.

Skimpy notes? You can tell you are not taking enough notes if a day or two later you look back at your notebook and can't seem to understand the connection between the words you have written down. You might look back at your history notes and see "1776," "let them eat cake," "Mao Tse-tung," and "Zapatistas." You seem to remember your teacher talking about revolutionary urges. But you don't remember the point he was trying to make or the connections he established, so these names, phrases, and dates are useless to you.

Overloaded notes? If you find you rarely look up or stop writing during class, you may be taking too many notes. "So what?" you may ask. "There's no harm in writing too much, right?" Wrong. Just as you should think critically as you read, so should you think critically as you listen. When you try to write down everything your teacher says, you are not really listening or thinking. You are not asking yourself questions, looking for connections, or evaluating the importance of what your instructor is saying. You are simply taking dictation. Furthermore, unless you know shorthand, you can't possibly write down everything. You might actually wind up missing something that is important because you were busy scribbling down something relatively minor.

Look at your notes honestly. Do you write down stuff you already know? Information that is already clearly covered in the textbook? Comments that are off the topic or have little to do with the class? If so, you are writing down too much. Your brain works much faster than your instructor's mouth or your pen. Use that advantage to make some judgments about what you are hearing.

What Your Instructor's Teaching Style Has to Do with Notes

The teaching styles your instructor uses and the kind of learning she expects from you (see chapter three) have a great influence on how many notebooks you are going to go through.

The Instructor Follows and Reviews the Textbook. You probably won't have to take heavy notes in this class as long as you keep yourself caught up with your assignments. The instructor is using class time to reinforce your reading and clear up any confusion. Don't feel like you need to write down anything that is already in the textbook. You will want to make note of what your teacher stresses as important, however. You can do this by marking your textbook as your teacher lectures (if you are allowed to write in it) or by keeping a list of "Important Concepts."

The Instructor Ignores Textbook, Lectures a Lot. This is a recipe for a hand cramp. If your instructor rarely covers material from the textbook—or doesn't give you a textbook at all—you may need to write down quite a bit and pay careful attention to organizing your notes (we'll give you tips on note organization shortly). The good news is that instructors who use this teaching style are often leaders in their fields who lecture based on many years of experience and research. Their classes can be very interesting.

The scary thing is that you feel like you are walking a tight rope without a net: If you miss something, how are you going to find it again? Strength in numbers is key. In chapter 6, we will talk about the many benefits of forming a study group. Filling in gaps in your notes is one of the perks study groups offer. If you can tell the class is going to be note heavy, buddy up as soon as you can.

Your Instructor Encourages Class Discussion of Assignments. Students read selections—short stories, philosophical treatises, historical essays, or whatever—and come to class prepared to discuss them. The instructor lectures for a little while to establish some context for the discussion and guides the talk by asking questions and providing more information as necessary. In classes like these, your focus will be on preparing notes on the reading before class so you can participate productively. During class, you will want to take notes on any background information your teacher gives and any useful ideas or viewpoints your classmates bring up. Since the focus of classes like these is interpretation, listening to and thinking about what your classmates have to say are more important than memorizing facts and dates.

Assessing Your Level of Mastery

Equally important to your teacher's style is your own level of skill in a particular area. Is literature one of those subjects in which you think you may be missing some "foundation"? Then you will probably have to take detailed notes in your literature classes. Are you a big Civil War history buff who has read two dozen books on the subject and could outline the strategy of every major battle? Undoubtedly, you won't have to take many notes when your Intro to American History instructor gets around to the 1860s.

You need to avoid two dangerous extremes when assessing your skills: being too cocky and being too insecure. Even if you do feel like an expert on a particular subject, don't check your brain at the door or leave your notebook at home. Even experts can learn something new now and then, and your teacher may provide some interesting facts or a new take on a subject. You may actually find out you know less than you thought you did; at the minimum, you will get a good review of a familiar subject. If, at the other extreme, you have the feeling that everyone else in the class knows more than you, get that negative, self-defeating thought out of your head. Believe us, everyone feels that way now and then, and they are usually wrong about themselves. Most likely, you know more than you think—and your classmates are probably just as nervous as you!

NOTE-TAKING TECHNIQUES AND TIPS

Note taking is very personal. There is no one correct way to do it. Don't worry—we're not trying to weasel out of giving you a system. We will give you a system we think works well. But you should feel free to customize it, improve on it, ignore parts of it, or come up with something that works better for you if you want. Give our system a try for a while, though—it got us through high school, college, and two graduate programs!

Note to Self

Tape Recorder Temptation

When you are low on confidence and your instructor is big on straying from the textbook, the idea of tape recording every lecture to give yourself some backup seems brilliant. Our advice is to leave the tape recorder at home. Why? First of all, it is almost impossible to avoid the temptation to let the machine do the listening for you. You slip into your old, inattentive ways, letting your mind wander and figuring, "Hey, I can always listen to the lecture later." That's pretty inefficient. You will have to spend an hour later listening to a tape to learn something you should have caught during the lecture. That's an hour you could have spent studying, sleeping, or doing whatever you pleased. Plus, you probably won't listen to the tape anyway. If you think it's hard to concentrate during a live class, try focusing on the droning, disembodied voice of your instructor coming out of a tape recorder. Second, your tape recorder doesn't capture any of the nonverbal cues your teacher gives to signal when he is giving important information, and it doesn't capture anything he writes down. Third, your tape recorder becomes a crutch that hampers the development of your listening and note-taking skills, both of which are vital to your success as a student.

Listen for Structural Clues

Wouldn't it be great if your instructor just handed you a written outline of his lecture ahead of time, with all the main point highlighted and all the supporting facts numbered in order? Actually, good teachers usually do give signals that let their listeners know what to expect from their lectures. They may be verbal signals instead of written signals, but if you know how to listen for them, you can take very clear, organized notes.

Make Sure to Listen to the Introduction. Here's yet another reason not to be late for class: In the first couple minutes of class, your teacher is likely to give a preview of what she intends to discuss. For example, let's say your teacher begins the class by saying, "Today we are going to cover the Spanish-American War: the events leading up to it, public reaction to the war in the United States and abroad, the results of the conflict, and the impact it had on U.S. diplomacy." In effect, your teacher has laid out a broad outline that you will be able to fill in as she lectures. First, she will cover the events leading up to the war, then the public reaction, then the results, and then the impact. Under each of those main headings, there will probably be several points and supporting points.

If your teacher doesn't lay out the lecture this way, use your syllabus, assigned readings, or other clues to predict the subject and possible structure of the lecture.

Catching the Main Points. Once your instructor begins the lecture, start listening for smaller structural clues. These clues can come in several forms. Here are the main ones:

- *A Set or Series.* Say, for instance, your teacher says, "There were three main factors that led the United States to declare war on Spain. . . ." *Three main factors.* A statement like that should have bells going off in your head. She is about to give you a numbered set of "factors" under the heading "events leading up to the Spanish-American War." Or say your biology teacher says, "The first stage of mitosis is . . . ." You can bet that a series of stages of mitosis are about to be covered. How convenient for you! You can number these sets and series as your teacher covers them. Just listen for numbers or numbering words (*"three* factors," *"first* stage," *"four* allies," etcetera).

- *Comparisons and Contrasts.* Many lecturers use comparison and contrast to make their points. Once you figure out what people or things they are trying to compare, you can structure your notes around them. For example, your instructor might say, "Henry David Thoreau and Ralph Waldo Emerson are two titans of American literature. Although they were friends who had much in common, they differed in many ways . . . ." Here, your instructor is setting up a comparison and contrast of Thoreau and Emerson. He will probably start listing characteristics of each, so what you need to do is set up a "Thoreau" heading and an "Emerson" heading, leaving room for supporting points under each. It's pretty easy to spot a comparison/contrast. Your teacher just usually comes right out and says, "Mitosis is like meiosis, except . . . ."

- *Chronology.* Your teacher may structure some portions of a lecture chronologically. For instance, instead of giving you a set of factors that led to the Spanish-American War, your teacher might prefer to explain the events that preceded the war in the order that they happened. Listen for dates and other clues about the passage of time (like "the next winter" or "one year later") and use them to structure those portions of your notes.

Use Page Layout Effectively

You can take a tip from your textbook publishers here: A good design helps make anything more readable and useful. You may want to use different layouts for different classes, depending on your needs.

A Classic: The Outline Format. If your instructor is a very organized lecturer who gives plenty of structural signals, the outline format is a natural choice. You have probably seen it before, but just in case, here's a quick review. Main section headings are marked with uppercase Roman numerals. Important points under each section are marked with capital letters. Supporting points under the important points are marked with Arabic (regular) numbers. Any points under those points are marked with lower-case letters. Indentation sets off each level from the other. A portion of your outline on the Spanish-American War might look like this:

I. Factors leading to the start of the Spanish-American War

    A. Increased American expansionism

        1. President McKinley platform included possession of Hawaii

        2. Plan for isthmus canal

    B. William Randolph Hearst

        1. Yellow journalism

        2. The De Lôme letter

        3. Support for Cuban insurrectionists

    C. Sinking of the *Maine*

You don't have to follow the rules exactly, but indenting and numbering this way helps you keep track of which points support which facts. Try at least indenting every time your teacher goes down another level of detail and using bullets or stars to mark sets of ideas. The outline is very skimmable, is handy when you need a quick review, and can be fleshed out easily.

Different Columns for Different Reasons. Setting up your notes in two or more columns is very useful in classes that rely on comparison and contrast. You simply draw a line down the middle of your paper and assign column headings that match the people or things being compared. Under each column, you may simply lists points of similarity and difference. If the lecture is more complicated, you might need to use a simplified outline format in each column.

Columns also work well if you often find yourself confused and left with unanswered questions. Divide your page lengthwise with a line, and take notes using the outline format (or some version of it) on the right. The left-hand column is what we call the "Huh?" column. As you outline a portion of the lecture, if questions occur to you or the instructor uses a word or mentions something you don't understand, write it down right across in the "Huh?" column. That way, you not only have a written list of questions and terms to clear up, you have a way of remembering what part of the lecture was giving you trouble. This makes it easier for your teacher to help you and for you to look up confusing information. For example, using the column format, the information from your Spanish-American War lecture might look like this:

	I. Factors leading to the start of the Spanish-American War
	A. Increased American expansionism
	• President McKinley platform included possession of Hawaii
What's an "isthmus canal"?	• Plan for isthmus canal
Why do we want one?	B. William Randolph Hearst
	• Yellow journalism
	• The De Lôme letter
Why did U.S. support Cuban revolution?	• Support for Cuban insurrectionists
	C. Sinking of the *Maine*

Map It All Out. A technique that writing teachers often use to help students brainstorm for and organize papers is called "idea mapping." You might want to give it a try as a note-taking system. The general concept is based on the metaphor of the tree: You have a central concept, which is like a trunk, with big branches—facts or points—shooting off of it. Smaller branches—supporting ideas—shoot off the big branches, twigs off the smaller branches, and leaves off the twigs. You don't have to draw a tree or anything, so don't panic. Just start by putting a main idea or heading down in the center of a page and circling it. As your teacher elaborates on the idea, start "branching out." Here's what that familiar section of our history lesson might look like:

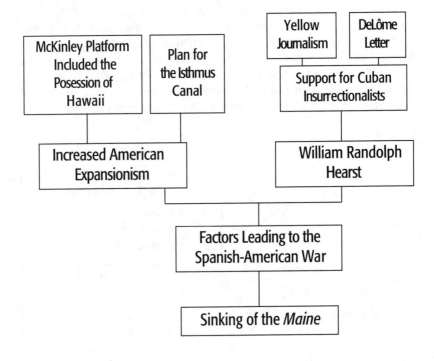

IDEA MAP

Idea maps are especially helpful for showing "the big picture" all at once. It is easy to see how many different events and people are related.

Making the Best of a Disorganized Lecture. Remember when we said that good lecturers give structural clues that help keep listeners oriented? Well, less organized lecturers, as you well know, often repeat themselves or digress. You probably will not be able to get a nice, neat outline out of them. Sometimes, you will be able to pick up structural clues, but you might wind up fooled: after announcing "three factors that led to the war," you may only ever hear about one. Or you may hear about one, then, 30 minutes later, hear about the other two. If this is the situation in one of your classes, do your best to organize your notes as you go, but realize that you might have to organize after the fact. You can do this by developing a highlighting system to mark main points, supporting points, definitions, and the like.

Say your history teacher briefly explains what "yellow journalism" is during your Spanish-American War lecture. You aren't sure what it has to do with anything, but you write down the definition anyway. Then, 15 minutes later, he proclaims that "yellow journalism," as carried out by William Randolph Hearst, was a factor in America's decision to declare war on Spain. At that point, go back and mark your "yellow journalism" section— underline it, put a star by it, or whatever. Just be consistent with your marking system, so later you know that you used a star to mean "important definition" and bullets to mean "series of related points."

Abbreviations R Yr Friends

No doubt about it, abbreviations can help keep the calluses off your note-taking fingers. You should definitely use them, and you should feel free to develop your own system of abbreviation. But first, read the following guidelines and pointers.

> ### *Did You Know...*
>
> *Participation Counts!*
>
> With the exception of gigantic introductory courses at college, class participation is an important part of your grade in most classes. We recommend that you participate in each and every one of your classes at least once every session by: asking a specific, thoughtful question, answering a question, or volunteering for something your teacher wants done (like reading a certain passage from the book out loud). Just once per class, that's all! Even if you're shy and even if you think you'll look like a geek. Take it from us, there are few things your teacher hates more than that awful, awkward silence that follows the asking of a question. Raise your hand and save her!

Leave out unnecessary articles, prepositions, verbs, and modifiers. If your political science teacher says, "Ross Perot is a billionaire from Texas who ran for president in 1992," you might write, "Ross Perot Texan billionaire ran president 1992." All you need to do is make sure you can translate your own notes later. Words like *a, an, the, in, for, or, at* or *to be* verbs (*was, are, is,* etcetera) are often not needed to keep the meaning clear. If any of the adjectives or descriptions are unhelpful to you, leave those out, too.

Cut letters from or shorten commonly used words. Instead of *can* write "cn." Instead of *point* write *pt.* Review notes you have taken in the past to find the handful of words that you use all the time, then shorten them. Be careful not to shorten everything on the fly. You may confuse yourself by using the same abbreviation for two very different words—like *pt* for both *point* and *part.*

If you find you are going to be using a long, unusual word or name over and over, come up with a short, easy-to-remember form of it. Instead of *Michelangelo*, write *Mich* or even *M.* Instead of *parthenogenesis*, write *parth.*

Use standard abbreviations and symbols. Here are some common abbreviations and symbols.

w/ = with	w/o = without
b/c = because	> = more than
< = less than	Δ = change
≈ = about, approximately	≠ = is different from
-> = led to, leads to	

KAPLAN

Review, Fill In, Rewrite

As soon as possible after class—definitely before the next class meeting—review your notes and make sure they are clear to you. This is especially important if you use a lot of abbreviations. Neaten up any handwriting that's so messy even you can barely read it. Explain in more detail any half-written notes. Clarify anything you think you might forget in a week or more. Make sure your notes have captured your understanding of the lecture.

After you have tidied up your notes, find the answers to any lingering questions. You can refer to your textbook, ask a trusted classmate, or ask your teacher. Don't let any questions linger until the next class session.

One terrific way to get the most out of your notes while building a useful study aid is to rewrite or type up your notes after class. One of the downfalls of notes is that they often seem perfectly clear a day or two after they are taken, but totally foreign and jumbled by the time you use them to study for your test. If you take the time to rewrite or type your notes, you can supplement them with information from your textbook and make sure they are perfectly organized. Some students get very creative with this and set up a color-coding system using pencils and markers. If you choose to do this extra step, you'll be giving yourself a helpful review and making yourself the most popular person in your study group—because you will have the best notes.

Chapter 5

Buying Time for Yourself

If you looked at other study guides before buying this one, you already know that almost every book on learning skills encourages readers to set up a study schedule. We will encourage you to do so, too. The difference, though, is that we have a healthy respect for your fun time, realistic ideas about how much studying you need to do, and, embarrassingly enough, an intimate familiarity with the problem of procrastination. We know how hard it is to set up a schedule and stick to it. In fact, all the tips and concepts we are about to outline we are actually using in our own lives right now—as we are writing this book.

Maybe you have tried designing a schedule for yourself before. Most people have. You stick to it for a few days, maybe a week, but important stuff keeps coming up that throws you off: you catch a cold, you have to pull an extra shift at your part-time job, you're having trouble with your girlfriend, or maybe there's a *Hawaii Five-O* rerun marathon on TV, and you just can't miss it (cable TV can really wreck a schedule, can't it?). So you rationalize the problem by saying, "Hey, this schedule thing is just too restrictive. I shouldn't have to force myself to study when I don't have 'the juice,' should I? I'll wait until I'm really in the mood." Of course, you will eventually be in the mood, but the mood is "panic" when you suddenly realize you haven't studied in three weeks and you have four tests coming up, and none of them are going to cover *Hawaii Five-O*. Or maybe you set up a schedule for yourself and really did try your hardest to follow it but wound up burned-out and exhausted after two weeks, convinced you just didn't have "what it takes" to succeed.

Believe it or not, in both of these situations, it was the schedule that was at fault, not you . . . Okay, maybe you were a little bit at fault, but only because you designed a schedule that didn't work for you. Coming up with a good, workable, effective schedule is not as easy as it seems. Designing the right schedule for yourself will require you to:

1. Make an honest assessment of your current time use.
2. Make an honest assessment of your study needs and powers of concentration.
3. Bargain with yourself to optimize fun time, which may be axing marginally fun stuff in favor of really fun stuff.
4. Keep yourself motivated by building rewards into your schedule and using the principle of "delayed gratification" (which we'll explain later).

If you think you can do these things, we can show you how to get yourself on schedule in just over a week.

Writing a book is a lot like studying. There are deadlines and demands, but it is up to the author or student to structure his time to fulfill those demands. The fact that you are reading this book proves that we successfully stuck to our schedule. And we'll let you in on a little secret: We made time for plenty of fun and relaxation while we did it. Let us show you how.

Try This

On a piece of paper, set up a week-long time grid like the one on the following page. For the next week, you will need to keep track of how you spend your time, so keep this paper in your pocket at all times. It's easiest to fill in your grid at least twice a day: at lunch, write down everything you did that morning, and before bed, write down everything you did in the afternoon and evening. Break your activities down into 30-minute increments, and include Saturday and Sunday in your schedule. For the next week, just live your life as you normally do. But be brutally honest on your grid! Remember, no one but you is going to see this.

A TYPICAL HIGH SCHOOL STUDENT'S ACTIVITY GRID

	MONDAY	TUESDAY	WEDNESDAY	THURSDAY	FRIDAY	SATURDAY	SUNDAY
6:30	Wake up, lie in bed	Wake up, lie in bed	Wake up, lie in bed	Wake up, lie in bed	Wake up, lie in bed		
7:00	Get up, shower, dress	Get up, shower, dress	Get up, shower, dress	Get up, shower, dress	Get up, shower, dress		
7:30	Eat, look for books, try to finish homework	Eat, look for books, try to finish homework	Eat, look for books, try to finish homework	Eat, look for books, try to finish homework	Eat, look for books		
8:00	Drive/ride to school	Drive/ride to school	Drive/ride to school	Drive/ride to school	Drive/ride to school		Wake up, shower, dress
8:30	Classes start	Classes start	Classes start	Classes start	Classes start		Go to church
9:00	Classes	Classes	Classes	Classes	Classes		
9:30	Classes	Classes	Classes	Classes	Classes		
10:00	Classes	Classes	Classes	Classes	Classes		
10:30	Classes	Classes	Classes	Classes	Classes	Wake up, wash face	
11:00	Classes	Classes	Classes	Classes	Classes	Look for something to eat	Come home from church
11:30	Classes	Classes	Classes	Classes	Classes	Eat sandwich, read magazine	Eat lunch
12:00	Lunch period	Lunch period	Lunch period	Lunch period	Lunch period	Call G., arrange meeting	Do yard work
1:00	Classes	Classes	Classes	Classes	Classes	Meet G. at gym, work out	
1:30	Classes	Classes	Classes	Classes	Classes		
2:00	Classes	Classes	Classes	Classes	Classes		Shower again

A TYPICAL HIGH SCHOOL STUDENT'S ACTIVITY GRID (CONTINUED)

	MONDAY	TUESDAY	WEDNESDAY	THURSDAY	FRIDAY	SATURDAY	SUNDAY
2:30	Classes	Classes	Classes	Classes	Classes		Catch up on anatomy; read while watching Green Bay game (volume low)
3:00	Classes end, go home	Classes end, go home	Classes end, go home	Classes end, go home	Classes end, go home	Go to mall, get corn dogs at Food Court, call B.	
3:30	Take a nap, hang out	Hit the gym	Eat sandwich, watch TV	Talk to L. on telephone, make plans for Fri.	Shoot some basketball		
5:30	Help with dinner	Go to mall and grab corn dog at the Food Court	Not sure what I was doing	Still on phone with L., until parents got home	Go to grocery store to pick up stuff	Rent movies, order pizza	
6:00	Eat dinner	Come home, start math homework	Order pizza, wait for pizza	Eat dinner	Help with dinner	Watch flicks, eat pizza	Eat dinner
6:30	Help with dishes	Math, still	Eat pizza, call B. and invite him over to study	Watch TV	Eat dinner		
7:00	Watch TV	Watch TV	Study with B.	TV	Get dressed for going out		Watch TV
8:00	Watch TV	Start history reading	Still hanging with B.	Middle of the Thursday lineup	Movie with B, L, G		
9:00	Do English reading	Call G and talk	Take a break, play some Game Boy	TV			Do Spanish homework
10:00	look at math assignment	Finish history	Study some more	Read anatomy book	Hang out with friends		Start English reading
10:30	TV	Go to sleep	More Game Boy	Still reading	Still hanging out		Sleep
11:30	sleep		B. goes home, sleep	Sleep	Head home	Head home	

ASSESSING YOUR CURRENT HABITS

Now that you have recorded your average week, let's analyze it. First, take a look at the sample activity record on the previous pages. Does your record look anything like this? You will notice that this student doesn't have a job or extracurricular activities. The student spends about 27 hours in class and also claims about nine at-home study hours. This brings up an interesting theory that students and working people alike have observed for years:

The Less Time You Have, the More You Get Done

Well, this isn't literally true. When people say "the less time you have, the more you get done," what they

> ### *Mind Boost*
>
> *Why Have a Schedule at All?*
>
> Why is scheduling your time better than doing things whenever the thought occurs to you? The best answer to that question is: because it saves you time and effort. Here's what we mean:
>
> - It is a hard fact that students who study at regular, set times spend fewer hours studying and get more out of their studies than students who study "whenever."
>
> - With a schedule, you face your responsibilities prepared and make fewer silly, time-wasting mistakes—like showing up at the library without the books you need. You know what to expect and you plan accordingly.
>
> - You gain a sense of control over your life, which lowers your stress level.

really mean is that the more structured your time is and the more you are forced to set aside certain times for certain tasks, the more you value your own time and the more you seem to accomplish.

We're not going to praise our example high school student too much. He could improve his habits in many areas. But the fact is, he can really study only in the evenings or on weekends, so even though you see him watching a lot of TV or talking on the phone, he is aware that he must get something done pretty much every night or be stuck doing everything on the weekend.

Does your time record show you spending more than two hours in a row watching television? Do you notice long periods of time spent just "hanging out"? Do you spend more than an hour at a time on the telephone? If so, your schedule is probably too free-form. You feel very little time pressure on a day-to-day basis and get less work done than you need to, but you don't realize it until test time. Test time provides the pressure that you don't usually feel. Once you are faced with a deadline, you immediately sense how valuable all your hours are—and begin to wonder what it was you were doing for all those weeks leading up to the test.

Do you have more than one extracurricular activity and/or a part-time job? You probably feel pressure all the time. You might even feel guilty when you are just relaxing—you have the feeling all the time that there is something you should be doing. Your time could be better managed to allow you the downtime you need.

Are You Really Studying?

Our example high school student invites his friend over one night to study. They take a pretty long break for Game Boy. Then they start studying again. Do you think they got a lot accomplished? Maybe, maybe not. This is just a made-up situation, after all. But think of your own habits. Do you ever get together with a friend or friends to study and wind up just talking and goofing off for most of the time you are together? It's a real temptation, especially if you aren't studying for a test the next day and don't feel pressured. Do you ever head to the library with your bag full of books, see a few people you know, chat for a while, wander around, people watch, and stare into space? You could easily blow several hours this way. Then there is the classic: "studying" with the television on. It is pretty much impossible, even with the sound down low. We hate to break it to you: None of these activities is really "studying."

Take a look at your activity record, and look for big blocks of time labeled "library" or "studying with Terry." Then ask yourself if what you were doing was really just hanging out in a studylike atmosphere. This messes you up in two ways: You don't really get any learning done (the purpose of studying) and you don't really have that much fun (the purpose of hanging out). As the saying goes, don't mix business with pleasure. When you study, study. When you hang out with friends, leave the books at home and have fun.

The Shockers

Were there some absolutely stunning wastes of time on your activity log? Our high school student spends two hours on the telephone discussing weekend plans. What about you? Did you spend two hours watching rebroadcasts of the World's Strongest Man Competitions from the late 1970s on ESPN2—and then stay tuned for their broadcast of the national sixth-grade spelling bee? (We were guilty of that one.) Did you spend an hour and a half arranging your socks by color? Did you go through your old magazines or comic books and wind up reading them again? Yikes!

Having a schedule will help you decide when activities like this are forgivable fun time or embarrassing avoidance techniques.

What's Required, What's Desired, What's Up for Grabs

Before you go on to designing your new schedule, you need to assess the importance of all the activities you are committed to right now, and the quality-of-life issues that are important to you. Some of your time is already scheduled and set. Some activities you want to do, but the times are not prescribed. Some of your hours are unscheduled.

What's Required. Your class schedule and work schedule are already set, either by you or for you. Practice time for sports and extracurricular lessons or activities are probably already scheduled, too. To a certain extent, your waking hours and sleeping hours may be set by these obligations. Say you have to be at

school at 8 A.M. and you know it takes you an hour to get ready and 15 minutes to get to school. You know you also need at least seven hours of sleep to feel rested. That means you need to require yourself to get up at 6:45 A.M. and go to bed before midnight. Everything else in your schedule will be worked in around these required activities.

What's Desired. Maybe you really want to have two hours, four times a week to spend at the gym. Maybe you want every Saturday completely free so you can go rock climbing. Maybe you love the free double-feature at the local theater every Thursday. These are regular activities that you enjoy and want to set aside time for.

"Quality of life" issues can also be desired. Maybe you want time to hang out with your friends and just relax every day. You might really value your afternoon gabfest or your midmorning smoothie break. Make a note of all these issues.

What's Up for Grabs. Every schedule needs a little flexibility. Stuff comes up that is impossible to schedule ahead of time—emergencies, random errands, a dream date with Will Smith, free tickets to Cancun with Gwyneth Paltrow. In your new schedule, your "up in the air" hours will give you the ability to shift responsibilities around. We'll explain more about that in just a minute.

DESIGNING THE PERFECT SCHEDULE

The perfect schedule is the schedule you can live with and stick to. It's a schedule that allows you to achieve all the goals that are important to you. We're going to help you design it right now, so get out a pencil and a pen and let's get cracking.

Blocking Out Your Time

First, get your list of desired activities and "quality of life issues." Then make a list of all your school subjects and about how much time each week you think you need to work on each one outside of class. On a time grid like the one you used before, mark off all the time blocks that are unchangeable in pen. Mark your waking and sleeping hours, too. Now, in pencil, mark in the activities you want to do but aren't required of you.

You should be able to see pretty clearly now how much time is left over. Before you start scheduling, ask yourself some important questions:

1. About how long can I read a difficult text before losing my concentration?
2. Are there certain subjects I really like or find easy?
3. Are there some subjects I can't stand or find difficult?
4. When am I at my sharpest mentally?
5. When am I at my dullest?
6. When do my friends usually stop studying and start wanting to hang out?

If your friends start coming by or calling every evening around seven o'clock, you will probably be really bummed out if you scheduled study time for seven (or, more likely, you will skip studying and go with your friends). If you hate calculus and you are fuzzyheaded in the morning, you won't be doing yourself a favor by scheduling your math study time at 8 A.M. Be aware of your strengths and weaknesses and try to schedule accordingly. And give yourself some breaks—more than three hours in a row of studying can break your brain!

Wouldn't it be wonderful if everything just matched up perfectly? If you were sharpest at 4 P.M. and you just happened to have that hour free for studying calculus? Or if your friends all had lunch at 1 P.M., and you had nothing else to do? Unfortunately, as you have probably already found out, things don't line up exactly right. You are going to have to make some compromises.

Bargaining With Yourself

You are going to have to buy your fun time by committing to study time. Set up your rewards in advance. Here's what we mean. Say on your "Quality of Life" list, you have "hang out with friends at least two hours a day." Say you also know that your friends congregate almost every night in the park at about

How Long Is Long Enough?

How many hours each week should you study outside of class? The answer depends on so many different variables, we couldn't possibly give you a hard and fast answer. The competitiveness of your school, the difficulty of your classes, and your familiarity with each of the subjects you are studying all play a role in study time. As a guideline, think of ten hours as your bare-minimum weekly study time. This is what you will need to commit to in order to stay on top of your workload. After analyzing your current study habits and your current performance in school, you will probably come to the conclusion that ten hours is not enough. You must find out for yourself how much time you require to perform as well as you want to in each class.

8 P.M., but they can also be found at Pete's Pizza most afternoons at 3 P.M. If your time were unscheduled, you might find yourself meeting up with everyone at 3 and doing nothing for the rest of the day and night. Instead, "buy" your hang time by committing to studying from 3 to 6 o'clock. You miss your friends in the afternoon, but come 8 P.M., you can put the books away and chill.

Maybe after school you can't face the books until you have played at least two hours of Sega. Well, do it—but realize that you are buying those two hours by giving up two hours of lame TV after dinner for studying. You get the idea here. Decide what's most enjoyable to you and figure out a way to give it to yourself by sacrificing something that is slightly less enjoyable. This may mean giving up (gasp!) Thursday night television because you want all of Friday afternoon off for soccer. You can't have everything. So make sure the activities you do keep are the choice ones.

What you will wind up with is a boilerplate schedule that has certain times blocked off for certain activities, but contains no specifics (like page numbers, assignments). Post it on your refrigerator or on your closet door or someplace where you can refer to it often.

Your Weekly "To Do" List

The schedule you have posted on your refrigerator (or wherever) tells you where you should be at what times, but it is basically blank. The events, chapters, papers, and assignments that will fill those blocks of time each week should go on a separate piece of paper: your "to do" list. You should make up

Playing dead might keep you from being eaten, but it won't make your work go away.

a "to do" list at the beginning of the week and either post it beside your schedule or carry it with you. We recommend breaking your list into big chunks—one chunk for every major responsibility (like "work," "school," and "personal"). Under each chunk heading, list all the tasks and subtasks you need to accomplish that week. As you accomplish each task, cross it off your list. Realize that you may have to add new tasks as they come up during the week.

Include big, upcoming projects. If, for example, you have a literature paper due in three weeks, you should probably already be thinking about it. Put "write paper" under your literature heading every week until it is due, and include at least one subtask under "write paper" each week—like "select topic" or "do library research." This keeps you aware that you need to be progressing toward completing the paper, and it makes it all the more satisfying to cross the big task off your list when you are finally done with it.

Break tasks down into smaller steps. This serves a double purpose. First, it forces you to think through the steps required in a project before you begin it. Second, it gives you lots

> **Mind Boost**
>
> *Switching to Plan B*
>
> Being flexible will help you make the best use of your time. For example, say you've decided to write an essay for your English class one morning, but you just can't get started. If possible, move on to another assignment. Let's say you also have to read an article for your next class in history. Do that instead of the essay. Commit to accomplishing something during your study hours, even if it's not what you originally intended to accomplish.

of stuff to cross off your list, which gives you a good sense of accomplishment.

TRICKS FOR STAYING MOTIVATED

In chapter 11, we are going to give you a set of quotes, lyrics, and movies designed to keep your burning urge to learn and succeed blazing like a bonfire. But on a week-to-week level, nothing keeps the flame going like good old-fashioned bribery. Actually, the more technical term is *delayed gratification*. Delayed gratification is eating your broccoli before allowing yourself that piece of chocolate cake. It's doing 50 pushups before you give yourself the Super Sport Quencher. It's promising yourself something you really want, and giving it to yourself, but only after you have completed some unpleasant or difficult task.

Build in a big reward for finishing big, nasty projects. Let's say you have a huge physics project due in a month, and it gives you a headache to even think about it. Promise yourself an all-day video marathon or a day at the lake or a big party as soon as you finish. Your reward doesn't have to be expensive. It just needs to be sufficiently tempting to keep you going. Put that big reward off to the side of the hateful task on your "to do" list each week. And keep thinking about it. The sooner you finish, the sooner you get your reward. If you can con your parents into bribing you, so much the better.

You can do this on a small scale with most tasks—just make sure the reward fits the task. For instance, you can promise yourself an hour watching your favorite TV show if you finish your homework before it comes on. Or you could promise yourself a cool new shade of fingernail polish if you get a B or better on your next math quiz. Don't go promising yourself a whole new outfit just for doing your English homework—it can't be that bad.

And don't be a big loser and cheat. You can't have your reward until you finish what you set out to do. Trying hard or almost finishing do not count.

Actually pay yourself. This is kind of a goofy trick, but we think it works. Most of your hanging out time is on the weekends, right? How much money do you usually spend? About 20 dollars? Here's what you need to do: Get yourself a big mason jar or coffee can and cut a slit in the lid. Now you have a kind of piggy bank. Get all your "weekend" money together at the beginning of the week and hide it in your sock drawer (or someplace where your sister won't steal it). Now set yourself an hourly "wage." The goal here is to "earn" all your weekend money by studying, so if your schedule demands ten hours of studying and you

KAPLAN

spend 20 dollars on the weekend, give yourself two dollars for every hour you work. Before you go to bed each night, "pay" yourself by taking the appropriate amount of money out of your sock drawer and putting it in your piggy bank. However much you end up with by Friday is how much you get to spend that weekend.

Okay, okay. We're not idiots. We know you're going to spend all the money in your sock drawer, even if you don't earn it all. But paying yourself is a fun, highly capitalistic way of symbolically motivating yourself through the week. After all, nothing better illustrates that "time is money" than the act of slipping those dollar bills into your mason jar. And you might even begin to feel guilty spending the money you didn't earn.

Chapter 6

Best-Kept Study Secrets Revealed!

If you have made use of all the tips you have read in this book so far, your battle for better grades is already half won. When test time comes around, you won't have gaping holes in your knowledge because of missed classes. You won't be scrambling desperately to learn weeks of material on your own in one weekend. You will have good, organized, complete notes. You will have done all assigned reading and homework. You will have paid attention in class. Now it is time to get down to the business of preparing for your exam.

THERE IS STRENGTH IN NUMBERS

Forming a study group is one of the smartest decisions you could make. It is such a good idea that in many law schools and graduate business programs—where everyone is a smart college grad—students are required to form study groups to help them through their difficult course work. Here are just a few of the benefits of group study:

- *You have a safety net.* If there are gaps in your notes or your understanding, probably at least one person in your group will be able to fill you in on what you are missing.
- *Group study keeps you motivated.* It's kind of like having a workout partner. Your group will encourage you, prod you, and expect results. And you are a lot less likely to blow off study time when you know other people are expecting you and counting on you.
- *Your group will keep you sane.* It is very reassuring to have a group of people who are in the same boat you are, facing the same deadlines. If you start to crack under pressure or freak out, they can put things in perspective for you—and you can do the same for them.

Did You Know...

Study Groups

Over one thousand people participated in our online poll about study groups. Here's how they responded.

Do you think they're useful?

66%   Yes
34%   No

Are you now in a study group?

76%   No
24%   Yes

Get In with the Right Crowd

Not all study groups are created equal. You have to select your partners with some care and make sure you suit each other. This means avoiding people who don't seem serious about working. Careless or disruptive students who miss class a lot or always show up late do not have a good attitude toward learning or respect for the class they are taking. They will be a dead weight in your group, mooching off you and expecting to get by with doing as little as possible. These folks may be a lot of fun to hang out with socially. You may even be friends with them. But don't mix business with pleasure—keep people who aren't serious out of your group.

You also want to avoid people who are way above or way below you in skill level in a certain class. This is not a comment on their character or yours. You will just get more out of your group if you share the same kind of concerns. The smartest student in the class will probably want to study less than you and will want to focus on different things. A struggling student will probably want to go over concepts that you have already mastered.

The biggest problem to watch out for is having too much fun in your group. Get a group of people with common interests together, and they wind up being friends. Get a group of friends together, and you wind up with a party. It is great if you make friends with your group members, but don't spend your study meetings goofing off, gossiping about your teacher, or talking about the movie you saw last weekend. Everyone in the group needs to agree that study time is sacred and that the discussion needs to stay focused on class business.

How, Who, When, and Where

How many people should you include in your group? We think three to five makes a nice size. If the group gets too much larger, not everyone can participate equally, and there is a tendency for subgroups to form. Having a group of two may not be ideal, but it is certainly better than nothing, so even if you can only find one person to team up with, do so.

If you already know several of the people in your classes, it shouldn't be hard to form a group. If you are new to a school, you might feel a bit awkward asking other students about working with you. Don't be shy. If you are a freshman, remember that most people in your classes are just as confused and worried as you are, and would probably welcome the chance to work with someone. Pick someone whose name you know, if possible. Maybe someone from your homeroom or someone you met during a field trip. Then just say, "Hey, do you want to try to get a study group together?"

Once you have your group set up, you need to organize regular meetings that everyone can attend. For really difficult classes with large work loads, you might want to meet once a week. For other classes, it is probably enough to set up one or two meetings before each test. You should meet some place that has few distractions and has a table you can all fit around. Libraries often have study rooms you can reserve for this purpose, but the dining room will work also.

Running Your Meetings

There are many different ways to run group meetings, and to a large degree how you and your group decide to organize your time together is up to you. But you must organize your time, and preferably in advance. In school and in the professional world, there is no bigger, more frustrating waste of time than a disorganized meeting. To avoid this problem, you should end each meeting by discussing what your plans are for the next meeting. This is called setting an agenda. When you have an agenda, everyone can arrive at your meeting prepared to be productive.

Here are some meeting models your group might want to try:

The Best Way to Learn Is to Teach. We don't know why this is true, but it is. When you are responsible for actively explaining something and taking other people step by step through a process, you are more likely to remember and master the material. Your study group can make use of this phenomenon by picking a different "group leader" for each session. It is the group leader's job to review class material, explain difficult concepts, and answer questions. This benefits the rest of the group, too, because they get to hear their lessons presented in different words and in a different way than their teacher presented them.

Question and Answer Session. You can ask each group member to come with a list of five to ten questions they had about the week's lessons. These can be questions they think might appear on a test or points of confusion for them. The rest of the group must answer these questions.

Quiz Popper. This is kind of like the "group leader" format. Each time, one group member must design a quiz on that week's material and give it to the group. The group takes the quiz, then the quiz popper goes over the answers and discusses them.

Design Your Own Test. This is a very useful exercise, whether you work with a group or alone. Before a big test, try to design at least one test that looks like what you think your real test will look like. Of course, this is easier after you have already taken one test in the class, but do your best even before the first test. How detailed will the questions be? What has your teacher been stressing? What will the format be? How tricky is your teacher? Take the answers to all these questions into consideration. You might use one study group meeting to design your test, and then use the next meeting to take the test and go over your answers.

STUDYING ON YOUR OWN

Even if you have a study group for every class, the majority of your test preparation time will be spent studying alone. For this, you need the right tools and the right mindset. We'll show you how to get both.

Alone in the "Zone"

Have you ever heard the phrase "in the zone"? It's a way athletes have of describing this weird mindset that takes them over sometimes, like an alternative reality in which they are not just their ordinary, talented selves, they are *Superheroes* who knock every ball out of the park, sink every basketball shot, run every pass in for a touchdown—you get the idea. They can't lose. It's like some eerie force has taken them over.

That is where you want to be when you are studying for a test. You have to put yourself in the "study zone" where you are no longer just a student worried about a test, you are an unstoppable learning machine, and academic force to be reckoned with. No facts are going to get by you. No concept is too difficult to understand. You are 100 percent sure that you are going to *crush* that test.

Mind Boost

Okay. You have a test coming up and you are ready to start studying. Where do you start?

- Start with everything, then narrow your focus to areas in which you need the most review.

- Gather all your class materials together: notes, books, graded homework, etcetera. Skim through it all attentively, looking for patterns in your mistakes (do you keep missing certain kinds of problems?) or gaps in your knowledge (still not sure about the difference between *meiosis* and *mitosis*?), and make a note of these gaps. Skimming attentively will refresh your memory on key points.

- Don't waste a lot of time focusing on stuff you already have down cold. Once you identify your weak spots, zero in on them.

Fear and insecurity are top causes of poor test performance. Many students don't wait until test day to have a big attack of nerves—they start panicking while they are studying. In fact, they spend more time worrying than studying, practically guaranteeing a bad test score. When you are in the zone, this can't happen to you. Fear and insecurity do not even touch you. Luckily, getting yourself into the "study zone" is a lot easier than batting .500 in the World Series or rushing for 300 yards in one football game. You just have to believe you are there, and you have to let go of any negative thoughts about yourself. Try actually saying this out loud a few times: "I'm in the zone. Nothing can stop me. I own this test. I'm all over it."

Does this sound totally corny? Well, it works. And if you won't take our word for it, just ask an athlete. He or she will tell you that confidence and faith in yourself are absolutely essential to success. And that is what "the zone" is all about: absolute confidence and faith in your ability to master the material and do well on your test.

Some Handy Study Aids

You are going to want to back up your supreme confidence with some tried and true study tools. Here a couple that have been favorites with students for generations—because they work:

A Last-Minute Study Sheet. You have reviewed your text, your notes, and your homework. You have focused on your weak spots. Now write or type out one neat, skimmable page that holds both the absolutely necessary, you-better-not-forget-them facts and any pieces of information you find yourself having difficulty remembering. On the day of the test, this sheet is all you will need to review.

Don't defeat the purpose of a study sheet by writing really small or using a tiny font so you can basically transcribe all your notes onto one page. Prioritize. And trust your brain to remember much more than is on that sheet.

Facts in a Flash. A deck of three-by-five flashcards has helped millions of students memorize countless facts. If your class is focused heavily on memorization, flashcards may be your best bet. Just buy a couple packs of blank note cards. On the unlined side, write a term, date, name, or phrase. On the opposite side, write out the definition or significance of that term, date, name, or phrase. Carry the deck around with you and periodically "flash" yourself a card, or have a friend do it. When you are sure you have mastered a card, take it out of the deck and put it in your desk. Your pile should get smaller and smaller as you approach test day.

How Do You Get to Carnegie Hall?

There's an old joke that goes like this: A tourist visiting New York City gets lost as he is looking for one of the city's best-known, most distinguished concert halls. He stops a man on the street and asks, "How do you get to Carnegie

Hall?" The man smiles and answers, "Practice, man. Practice." In studying for a test as in launching a career in music, there is no substitute for plenty of practice. In fact, if your class focuses mainly on application or interpretation skills, most of your study time should be devoted to practice.

If you are preparing for an "application" test (a math test is a prime example), do as many practice problems as you can—old homework problems, sample questions from your textbook, questions you make up yourself. If you are preparing for an "interpretation" test (a literature test is a prime example), practice looking for specific similarities and differences between the different works (poems, stories, books, art works, historical periods, or whatever), and then drawing conclusions based on those similarities and differences. Just pick any two works and ask the same set of questions about both. Mix and match all the different works and practice writing a compare-contrast paragraph about each pair.

THE PERSISTENCE OF MEMORY

No matter what kind of test you are preparing for, you will probably have to memorize something. Maybe lots of things—especially if you are getting ready for a science test. Flashcards are great, but there are a few more tricks you can use.

Sing Out Loud. It's pretty easy to remember music lyrics, right? Try singing some fact, formula, definition or series to the tune of one of your favorite songs—or make up a suitable tune of your own. This can often prove hilarious, especially if you use a song that is being played a lot on the radio right now. What will happen is you'll get the song stuck in your head—but with your new lyrics. Don't worry about rhyming anything. Just sing the words you want to remember.

Give It Rhyme or Rhythm. This is for the tone deaf. You can get the same benefits of songwriting by rephrasing an important piece of information so it has rhyme and/or rhythm. One example of this you have probably heard is, "In fourteen hundred and ninety-two/Columbus sailed the ocean blue." It is not necessary to give something both rhythm and rhyme, and your rhymes don't necessarily have to make perfect sense. For instance, if you wanted to remember the name of the battle that devastated Napoleon, you might say, "Napoleon turned blue at Waterloo." The rhyme and rhythm make each fact far more memorable.

Visualize Something Weird or Funny. Try to come up with an image that reminds you of the fact you are trying to memorize. To remember Napoleon's defeat at Waterloo, for example, you might picture Napoleon going down the toilet—there is water in the toilet, some people call the toilet the "loo," and the fact that he's in a toilet will remind you that he was defeated in the Battle of Waterloo.

Use Sound-Alike Words. This works well for foreign language tests, especially if combined with a visualization technique. For example, if you are trying to remember that the Spanish word *trabajar* means "to work," try to think of something *trabajar* sounds like. It is pronounced "trah-bah-HAR," which kind of (sort of) sounds like "travel far," right? If you picture a traveling salesman with a suitcase or an airline pilot, you can associate working with "travel far," which will make you remember *trabajar*.

The Classic: Acronyms. Acronyms are words formed from the first letter or letters of a group of words—like SCUBA, which stands for *self-contained, underwater breathing apparatus.* You can use acronyms to help you remember a series or set of facts. Sometimes you can't make the acronym into a real word, but as long as you can kind of pronounce it, it works. An example you probably already know is the name "Roy G. Biv." This is an acronym for the colors of the spectrum: red, orange, yellow, green, blue, indigo, violet.

If you can't make a word with the first letters of the series of words you want to remember, try making a new sentence that uses those letters. Music students learn the sentence "Every good boy does fine" to remember what notes go on the lines in the treble clef (E, G, B, D, and F). If you were trying to memorize the different levels of classification scientists use to categorize animals, you would be trying to learn: Kingdom, Phylum, Class, Order, Family, Genus, Species. That's not easy to remember, and neither is the acronym KPCOFGS. But you could easily remember the sentence "King Philip cooks omelets for good servants."

Ask Your Friends to Quiz You. If there are just a few pesky facts and figures you can't seem to memorize, ask your friends' help. Give each friend a different question and answer. Every time they see you or call you, they have to ask you that question.

BEATING THE BRAIN BUSTERS

Studying for a test can be lonely, difficult work, even if you are very well prepared. Sometimes, despite your best efforts, the brain busters seize you: boredom, fatigue, and headache. Remember, the chances of your winding up numb, exhausted, and in pain at two in the morning will be minimized if you stay on top of your work. But just in case, here are some general things you can do to keep your motor running:

Watch Your Posture. When you are studying, sit in a chair that is comfortable but fairly stiff. You want to keep your back straight and your shoulders relaxed. Slouching or hunching over can cause your shoulder and neck muscles to tense up, which will give you a nasty headache.

Don't Squint. Make sure you have plenty of light and appropriate glasses. Squinting can also bring on a headache. So can frowning or scowling—two expressions many students wear when they study. Try to keep your jaws and face relaxed. A good way to force your face to relax is to get up and brush your teeth. It loosens up your cheeks and jaws. And it clears up that nasty coffee breath!

Limit Yourself to One Caffeinated Drink After Dinner. Speaking of coffee breath, steer clear of the java, soda, or over-the-counter "pep" pills after dinner. You can have one night-time cup or glass if you really must, but only one. Take it from a couple of reformed coffee addicts: You will want to sleep eventually, whether you have been caffeinating yourself or not. Your brain can stand only so much, and sooner or later, it will demand rest. If you have been good and stayed away from the coffee and soda, you can slip off to dreamland

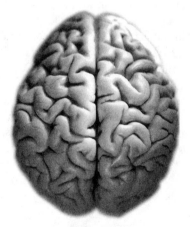

Give your brain a break.

peacefully when your brain tells you it's quitting time. If you have been bad, your brain will be begging for sleep, but your body will be an unwilling, jumpy mess. You won't get any more studying done and you won't get any sleep, so you will be good and tired and cranky when you face your test. Not very smart.

Go to Bed, for Heaven's Sake. Those people who drag themselves in to class on test day looking like hammered dog food and moaning about the all-nighter they pulled should be pitied. But do not go admiring them for their dedication. Panic and insecurity are what really led them to stay up all night. They probably did not get anything much accomplished. If you have stayed caught up and started studying for your test at least a few days ahead of time, there is no reason for you to burn the midnight oil the night before the test. The best favor you can do yourself is to get a good night's sleep so you will be especially perky and bright-eyed the next day.

Take "Power Breaks." If the subject you are studying is so dry or complex it makes your skull shrink, don't try to study too much in one sitting. Concentrate for as long as you can—at least one hour—then take a ten-minute power break. A power break is not like a regular break. Do not turn on the television, call a friend, or even talk to someone. Just get up, leave your study area, and do something mildly physical while letting your brain go blank. Walk briskly around the block. Do jumping jacks, sit-ups, or stretches. Punch a punching bag (if you are lucky enough to have one). Don't think about the material you are studying for those ten minutes. You are basically "resetting" your brain so you can start studying again.

Do not get involved in any conversations on your break. Since you don't like what you are studying, anything will distract you from it. If you see a friend coming your way, just say, "Can't talk now. I'm in the zone." They will understand.

Okay, now you have some heavy guns in your arsenal: great class attendance and participation, solid work habits, and top test-preparation techniques. Let us show you how to marshal your forces on test day.

Tackling the Test

Most of what is involved in doing well on tests has already been covered in this book: good study habits, listening, and concentration. Still, there is certainly a lot to be said for developing good test-taking skills, too. Ever heard of the SAT, for example? (What are we, crazy? Of course you have—and we'll talk more about it at the end of this chapter.) Many critics of this test claim that it does not measure students' knowledge, but actually tests their "test-taking abilities." That is, your score on the SAT doesn't show how smart you are, it shows only how good you are at taking the SAT. Despite the fact that there are some logical holes in this argument, it does contain a kernel of truth. The fact is, any exam is partially a test of your ability to do well on that type of test. It is possible for one student to have studied and prepared less than another and still do better on a test merely because she is a more capable "tester."

Not fair, you say? You are probably right. It really isn't fair to reduce a student's body of knowledge and breadth of skill to a single number or letter. Unfortunately, the only practical way educators have found so far of measuring students' abilities is through tests, all of which are standardized to some degree or another. You will have to face them throughout your academic life, and perhaps even in your career. The good news is, test-taking skills can be learned, just like any other set of skills. This chapter lays it all out for you.

PSYCH UP, NOT OUT

As we mentioned in the last chapter, the number-one enemy of test takers is nerves. Text anxiety has struck most people at one point or another. Believe it or not, straight-A students are especially prone to it. You know what we're talking about, right? As soon as that bell rings on test day and you hear the phrase, "You may now begin . . .," your pulse starts to race, your stomach flip-flops, and everything you had memorized flies out of your head. You frantically rush through the test, making countless careless mistakes you would never have made under different conditions. The test period ends, and you are nowhere near finished. You leave feeling worthless and depressed.

Part of the problem is simple jitters. Part of the problem is lack of confidence. Let's examine both.

Try This

Are You A Stressed Tester?

Even if you don't have the exaggerated symptoms we described above, you still might suffer from test anxiety. Ask yourself the following questions:

1. Do you think that most other students are smarter or more capable than you are?
2. Do you feel that trying hard in school is basically a waste of time because you'll never really be able to make better grades anyway?
3. Do you ever refer to yourself as "stupid"?
4. Do other people ever call you stupid?
5. Do you feel a lot of pressure from your parents to excel in school?
6. Do you worry that if you don't make all A's and B's, your life will be ruined?

If you answered "yes" to any of these questions, you could very well be psyching yourself out before tests or worrying in a way that will hurt your performance.

Low Self-Esteem

The root of the most destructive form of text anxiety is a feeling of academic inadequacy. Because of past problems in school, negative comments from others, or your own uncertainties about yourself, you might have it in your head that you just can't excel. On test days, you defeat yourself before you even try because you are convinced you will fail. This is what is called a self-fulfilling prophecy: You believe you will fail so, subconsciously, you make yourself fail. Bad thoughts about yourself will only hold you back, so do yourself a favor and start trying to get over all the negativity. What you need to be happy and successful—and not just on tests, either—is a big, healthy dose of self-confidence. If you feel good about yourself, you will believe you can succeed. That's the kind of self-fulfilling prophecy you are looking for. Here are some steps to take to get you on the road to self-esteem.

Who Loves Ya, Baby? A bunch of people, probably. Not to get all mushy or anything, but think about all the family members and friends you have who care about you and would go the extra mile for you if you needed them. People who love you don't think you are dumb or worthless. They believe in you, so why shouldn't you believe in yourself? Identify the people in your life who really have your happiness at heart, and hang out with them more often.

Cut Those Jerks Off. Do you spend time with someone who cuts you down or makes you feel inadequate? Stop! People who try to make themselves feel better by putting others down are jerks, and your time is too valuable to be wasted on them.

Ask for the Right Kind of Encouragement. Sometimes, in an effort to help, parents, friends, brothers, and sisters actually wind up hurting you. They may think they are encouraging you by putting your performance in school down or telling you you aren't doing a good enough job—kind of like a coach might yell at his players. This tactic will not help you in school. When you are feeling calm, approach your family member or friend in a polite way and explain that you really do want to do better in school and you would appreciate their help. Then explain the help you want: someone to keep telling you that you can and will excel, to praise you when you do well, and to help you look on the bright side when you slip up. If they keep up their old ways, just remember, they probably are trying to help. Ignore their negative messages and focus on the fact that they are interested in you and your future.

Confidence Is Attractive. People who are sure of themselves and their abilities are very attractive. You have probably noticed this. Even people who aren't all that good looking seem to get a lot of attention as long as they act like they feel good about themselves and their abilities. Okay, so this doesn't have much to do with doing well at school, but it's a nice bonus of high self-esteem, don't you think?

Back in "The Zone"

Building high self-esteem can be a long-term process. But there are also some important tactics you can use to psych yourself up and keep your palms dry and your stomach butterfly-free. The ideal frame of mind on test day is "alert, calm, and comfortable."

Don't Change Your Routine. Sometimes, when faced with a really big test like a final or the SAT, students are tempted to do weird things to prepare, like sleep for 20 hours, swallow raw eggs, or down a bucket full of spaghetti. Hey, you are taking a test, not running a marathon. Don't do anything extreme that will upset your equilibrium. If you usually jog three miles a day, don't jog eight in an attempt to burn off extra stress—you'll wind up exhausted and sore. If you usually sleep six hours a night, don't force yourself to stay in bed for ten—you'll be sluggish.

Make Sure You Have Your Supplies Lined Up. Get everything you need together the day before the test. That means two pencils or pens (in case one breaks), a exam blue book if your instructor requires one, your calculator, or whatever else you are supposed to have on hand. Put all of those things in your book bag, and put your book bag by the door. Nothing will blow your cool faster than showing up for the test and then realizing you don't have a pen or searching frantically for your graph paper only minutes before the test starts.

Stay In the Zone! Keep yourself focused and keep telling yourself that nothing can stop you. You own this test! You will crush it into tiny bits! You laugh at this test and its puny attempts to trick you, because you are unbeatable!

KAPLAN

Be Prepared for the Sahara Or the Tundra. Why is it that when it is cold outside, classrooms are blazing hot, and when it is hot outside, classrooms are like the Arctic? Are the maintenance people pulling some kind of sick joke? On the day of the test, you want to make sure you won't be distracted by your own chattering teeth or the sweat dripping into your eyes. Dress so you will be completely comfortable. If you are not sure what the classroom temperature will be like—which will most likely be the case when you go take a standardized admissions test—wear a short-sleeved shirt (in case it is hot) and bring along a warm sweater (in case it is cold).

THE INTERPRETATIVE, OR "ESSAY," TEST

The term "essay test" strikes fear into the hearts of many students. They know that many upper-level courses rely on essay tests, which makes that format seem more advanced. They also know that essay tests will require them to write clearly and effectively—and that terrifies a lot of people. Sure, essay tests can be tough. But they have their bonuses. Essay tests give you much more control over your answers. Think about it this way: On a fill-in-the-blank test, if you don't know the answer to a question, you miss it. You can't say, "Well, I don't know that fact, but I do know all these other facts that you didn't ask me about!" On an essay test, you get to decide how to support yourself. You decide what facts are important. Your essay must be reasonable and well grounded, but as long as you show that you know what you are taking about, you get credit. Not bad, huh?

> ### *Note to Self*
>
> *Wear A Watch*
>
> If your classroom doesn't have a plainly visible clock, wear a watch to your test. This is extremely important. You will need a watch in order to budget your time effectively and complete all parts of the test successfully.

Time, Time, Time

The clock is your master. Obey it. At the start of each essay test, assess the task ahead of you and come up with a reasonable plan of attack that will allow you to complete every section of the text satisfactorily.

Pencils down!

The most serious, unnecessary mistakes on essay tests are the results of poor time management. These are rookie mistakes, like spending precious minutes worrying about some unimportant fact, or misreading questions because you were in a rush, or failing to finish the test because you spent all your time on one question. During each exam, the smart tester makes time for several important steps:

Read Through the Test. Read the directions carefully, underlining important requirements like "answer two out of three" or "compare and contrast." Quickly, but carefully, read through the questions. If you are given the option of choosing which questions you want to answer, you should mark the ones you feel most comfortable with. By reading through the test, you ensure that you understand the task and roughly how much time each stage of it will take. You don't want any surprises once you start writing, like some mandatory, complicated question at the end of the test that you left no time to answer.

Map Out and Schedule Your Attack Plan. Decide which questions you will answer, or, if you have to answer all of them, decide in what order you want to answer them. Instructors don't mind if you answer questions out of order as long as you number them clearly. If you have studied hard, it is likely you would be capable of answering any of the questions. Pick the ones you think you can answer most thoroughly in the limited time you have.

Next, budget your time and arrange your questions according to difficulty or complexity. If the questions are all about the same, you can assign equal amounts of time to them. If one question is harder or longer, give it some extra time. If the questions are all given equal weight, start with the easiest. If one question is worth most of the points on a test, start with it. Your attack plan should include time for organizing, outlining, writing, and proofreading.

Organize and Outline. Before you start to write your answer to any question, jot down the key points and facts you think your response should include. You can do this on the back of the test sheet. Then make an outline that puts those ideas and points in a logical order. The standard structure for an essay response is the "five-paragraph" structure—a format that has been taught be writing instructors and used by students for literally hundreds of years. Until you have mastered spur-of-the-moment essay writing, you should probably stick to this structure:

I. Introduction—You briefly outline the direction your argument will take, without including specifics. List three main points you will illustrate.

II. Point One

    A. Supporting fact

    B. Supporting fact

III. Point Two

    A. Supporting fact

    B. Supporting fact

IV. Point Three

    A. Supporting fact

    B. Supporting fact

V. Conclusion—Make a final statement that pulls together all your points, but don't restate the introduction.

The way you order your points is up to you. Some people like to lead with their strongest, most compelling idea, and follow it with smaller points. Others like to finish with a bang by saving their main point for last.

Write Your Response. Don't worry about writing an elegant response that sounds like poetry. Unless you are a very gifted writer, you will not be able to craft a Pulitzer Prize–winning essay in 30 pressured minutes—in fact, most gifted writers would not be able to, either. Your instructor understands this. What she is looking for is independent thought expressed clearly, neatly, and correctly. You can definitely live up to this standard, even if you do not think you are the strongest writer. The key is to write a response built on simple, direct, specific sentences that follow each other logically and are free of grammatical errors. Here are some basics:

- To keep yourself on track, make only one point per sentence, and keep each sentence short—no more than four handwritten lines. Think of the kind of writing you usually find in newspapers. That is the style you are after.

- Avoid semicolons, exclamation marks, and parenthetical statements. Many people use semicolons incorrectly and exclamation marks too frequently. Parenthetical statements can knock your sentence off track. Stick to commas, periods, question marks, and maybe an occasional dash.

- Keep your writing free of fragments and run-ons. These are two common grammatical errors that can destroy your credibility as a writer. A fragment is an incomplete sentence and a run-on is two or more sentences jammed together without proper punctuation or linking words. These errors should be easy to avoid if you keep sentences short and proofread carefully.

- Back yourself up every step of the way. When you make an assertion, use specific facts, quotes, or information you learned in class to support your statement.

- Use transitions to smooth out your writing. A choppy but clearly written essay is acceptable, but your instructor will be more impressed if you smooth out the flow between sentences and paragraphs using transition words and phrases.

- Be formal, but not stuffy. Don't try to impress your teacher by using puffed-up language or unnecessarily long words. You will just muddle your meaning and wind up looking silly. At the same time, do not use slang, contractions, or curse words. No matter how strongly you feel about something, do not call it a "piece of ___ " in your essay.

- Skip every other line as you write, and mind your handwriting. Skipping lines not only makes your response easier for your teacher to read, it gives you a little room to add information if you need to. Try to keep your writing legible. If your cursive looks like squiggles, try printing instead.

Proofread Your Response. Your schedule should include enough time to check your responses carefully. One technique we recommend is moving your lips while you read—that is, pretending you are reading out loud, but not making a sound. This helps you "hear" your sentences inside your head, which makes spotting grammatical errors easier. It also slows you down a little, which will help you catch other mistakes or gaps.

How Much Time Should Each Phase Take? How much time you decide to spend on each phase of answering an essay question depends on many factors, including its level of difficulty and your own skill. Here is a sample breakdown of a common test situation:

> ── *Mind Boost* ──
>
> *Making a Transition*
>
> Some helpful transitions include: *as a result, because of this, for example, furthermore, however, in addition, in comparison, in contrast, meanwhile, more importantly, nevertheless, not only . . . but also, on the other hand, since.*

- You read the directions and discover you must answer three out of five test questions in your one-hour test period, and that all questions are worth the same amount of points. Time spent: 1 minute

- Your read through all the essay questions, noting the ones that you feel you could answer quickly and confidently. Time spent: 3 minutes

- You pick the three questions you like best, and decide which one is easiest and which one hardest. Time spent: 1 minute

- Organize, outline, and write your first response. Time spent: 15 minutes (no more than 3 minutes on organizing and outlining)

- Organize, outline, and write your second response. Time spent: 15 minutes

- Organize, outline, and write your third response. Time spent: 15 minutes

- Proofread your responses. Time spent: 10 minutes

Some Other Pitfalls of Essay Tests

Aside from poor time management, two common mistakes students make on essay tests are "data dumping" and "regurgitating." Neither tactic will earn you high marks.

Data dumping means including absolutely every fact, every quote, and every piece of information you have learned so far in your essay response. What's wrong with that, you ask? Nothing, as long as all those facts are relevant and help clarify your response. The problem comes in when students throw in everything but their mother's maiden name, whether it is on the topic or not. This is problematic for several reasons. First, it wastes your valuable time. Second, it can make you look like you don't know what you are talking about—like you are just throwing out facts and hoping some of them are on target. Third, it can make you look like you don't have enough judgment to know what is important and relevant and what isn't. Fourth, it makes for terrible, clunky essays that are difficult to follow.

Mind Boost

Stumped or Out of Time?

But what if you do run out of time? Or what if you have absolutely no idea how to answer one of the required questions? Those are pretty big problems, but all is not lost. See chapter ten for what to do when everything goes wrong.

We understand the motivation behind many data dumps: You studied hard, and you want it to show. You want your instructor to know just how many facts and quotes and names you memorized and pondered. Resist this temptation. Part of what you are being tested on, remember, is your ability to do well on an essay test. That means exercising some discretion and using only the facts that strengthen your argument.

Regurgitating means just spitting up the exact words and phrases your instructor has been using and introducing no ideas of your own. This is desirable on an application- or memorization-based test, but on an interpretive test, you are expected to make and support your own arguments. You probably won't be failed for regurgitating, but you will not make a higher grade than a C.

SHORT-ANSWER AND FILL-IN-THE-BLANK

Depending on how tough your teacher wants to be, short-answer (which usually means one or two sentences) and fill-in-the-blank tests can be harder than essay tests or multiple-choice tests. On an essay test, you can play to your strengths. On a multiple-choice test, you at least have a chance of guessing the correct answer. But on a short-answer test, you have very little leeway. You have to come up with a specific answer from memory.

There are two techniques you can use to maximize your score on these types of tests: triage (pronounced "TREE-ahzh") and clue detection.

Triage on the Testing Ground

After a battle, when there are so many wounded soldiers brought into a field hospital that they can't all be treated at once, military doctors use a method called "triage" to decide who should be looked after first. They divide the wounded into three groups (three from *tri*): the slightly wounded, the seriously wounded, and the ones who will probably die. In most cases, the ones who look like goners are attended to last because the doctors figure they will save more lives (and return more people to battle) if they pay attention to the other two groups.

It is a pretty grim metaphor, but you can use it to plan your "treatment" of short-answer, fill-in-the-blank, and even multiple-choice tests like the SAT or ACT. You break the test questions into three categories: the ones you know right away, the ones you might have to think about for a minute, and the ones that stump you. The point of this technique is to help you answer as many questions as possible without getting hung up on one question that, in the end, you might simply not know. Many students lose their cool when confronted with

Don't give every test question the same treatment.

a question they can't answer. They stop and think and think, getting more and more nervous. Several minutes tick by while they could have been answering plenty of other questions whose answers they knew in a heartbeat. Triage helps you avoid this problem.

Here is how the method works:

1. First, go through the test quickly but carefully, answering only the questions you know right away. If you have to spend more than ten seconds thinking about a question, but you think you know the answer, put a little mark by the question and skip it for now. If a question baffles you, don't freak out. Just skip it.

2. After you finish your first run through the questions, go back and attend to the questions you marked. These are questions you will have to think about for half a minute or so. But be careful not to let the time get away from you! If you have to think about the question for more than a minute or two, move on.

3. Once you finish the second run through, you can start treating the stragglers—those few questions you are having trouble with. If you have even the slightest clue about one, focus on it for a while. As time runs out, take your best guess at the remaining questions.

   We have said it before, but it is worth repeating: be aware of the time. If you have 20 questions to answer in 60 minutes, you just can't afford to spend 15 minutes on one.

Clue Detection

Have you ever watched the television game show *Jeopardy!*™? Ever wonder how the contestants seem to be able to answer those difficult questions faster than you can even read them? The secret is, they often aren't really reading the whole question. There is usually a simple clue in the questions that helps them figure out the answer without even considering the whole question. Your instructor will often put clues in your short-answer or fill-in-the-blank questions, too.

For example, let's say you ran into this question: "This man said, 'We must all hang together, or assuredly we will all hang separately.'" There is little to go on there. But what if the question read, "On July 4, 1776, this man said, 'We must all hang together, or assuredly we will all hang separately.'" Now there is a clue: July 4, 1776. What is special about that day? It is the day the Declaration of

Independence was signed by our founding fathers, an act considered treasonous by the British government. So you can probably assume that the answer to the question is one of the signers of the Declaration of Independence. This one clue might jog your memory, causing you to recall that it was, in fact, Benjamin Franklin.

Let's try another example. Say a question read, "What president instituted a 'lend-lease' program to aid the British in their war effort?" All you have to go on is "lend-lease" and the fact that Britain was at war. But what if the question read, "In his third term, this president instituted a 'lend-lease' program to help the British fight the Nazis." Now you have something to go on. Even if you don't know a thing about the "lend-lease" program, you know you are being asked for the name of a third-term president who was in charge during World War II. You may know that the only president in U.S. history to serve more than two terms was Franklin D. Roosevelt, or you may remember that Roosevelt was president at the beginning of World War II. Either way, you can use the clues to answer the question.

Don't be thrown off if you don't know the specific piece of information the question is asking for. Look for the hidden questions within the questions whose answers you do know.

MULTIPLE-CHOICE TESTS

Teachers like multiple-choice tests because they are very easy to grade. The cool thing about them from a student's perspective is that the answer is *right there staring you in the face*. All you have to do is figure out how to distinguish the right answer from all the wrong answers. If you know the answer, this is easy. It's when you are not sure—or don't know at all—that things get tricky. There are some tactics you can use.

> ### *Note to Self*
>
> Math problems are akin to short answer in that one specific answer is being looked for, but also like essay questions in that your teacher wants to see how you got from one point to another. Always show your work. Even if you wind up with the wrong answer in the end, your teacher is likely to give you partial credit if you got some of the calculations right.

Good Old Trusty Process of Elimination

When you go shopping for clothes, isn't it easier to spot what you don't like than something you like? The same can be true with multiple-choice questions. The wrong answers jump right out at you. For example, look at this question:

1. At what speed does light travel?

   a. 10 miles per minute

   b. 186,300 miles per second

   c. 5 inches per hour

   d. 201 miles per second

Maybe you haven't a clue about the speed of light. You know it must travel pretty fast. All you know, from watching *Star Trek*, that a light-year is a very long distance. Even if you haven't memorized the speed of light, you can probably eliminate answer choices "a" and "c." So you are left with 201 miles per second and 186,300 miles per second. You are pretty sure, based on what you have seen on television, that the speed of light must be over 1,000 miles per second, so you eliminate "d." The only answer left is "b," which is, in fact, the correct answer. Using the process of elimination, you could answer this question correctly by knowing the wrong answers.

Eliminate an answer only if you are reasonably sure that it is wrong. You don't want to be too hasty and cut a correct answer just because it is unfamiliar to you or you don't know what it means.

Mind Boost

Are We Repeating Ourselves . . . Again?

Yes, we are. On a multiple-choice test, as on any test, you must budget your time and read directions carefully. Don't get hung up too long on any one question, and use the triage method (explained earlier in this chapter) to maximize the number of points you earn.

KAPLAN

Give It a Guess

Let's return to the example above. What if the answer choices read like this:

    a. 10 miles per minute   b. 186,300 miles per second

    c. 5 inches per hour   d. 136,800 miles per second

If you didn't know the answer, process of elimination would narrow the field down only to "b" and "d"—both seem possible. Now what do you do? Eeny-meeny-miney-mo?

It depends. If there is no penalty for wrong answers—that is, if you just get a zero for a wrong answer and your teacher doesn't actually deduct points from your score—*always, always* guess. You have nothing to lose. If you leave it blank, you will get zero points, but if you guess, you just might guess right.

If your teacher counts off points for wrong answers (and many do this to discourage guessing on a multiple-choice test), you should guess only when, statistically, you stand to gain from guessing. Your statistical probability of gaining points can be difficult to calculate when you are under pressure, so a good rule of thumb is, *only guess when you can eliminate at least one answer choice* (out of four), *and don't guess on more than one third of the questions.*

In case you are curious about the reasoning behind this, it's all about the odds. Let's say your teacher gives you two points for every correct answer, but subtracts one point for every incorrect answer. There are 20 questions on the test, each with four answer choices, and you have answered 12 of them correctly. You are puzzling over the last eight. If you guess blindly, you have a one-in-four chance of answering each question right. That means the odds are, you will answer two questions right by chance, but miss six. If you eliminated one answer choice from each question and then guessed, you might answer three questions correctly, gaining one point overall. If you can eliminate two choices from each question, you have a 50-50 chance of answering any question correctly. You would probably gain four points.

Some Multiple-Choice Pitfalls

There are a few common problems that can throw off the multiple-choice test taker:

Decoys. Stay on your toes. Your instructor may try to lure you in with an answer that looks like a "gimme." If you look at the answer choices and think, "Well, that's obvious," think again. For example, if your teacher asks:

3. Who wrote *The Autobiography of Miss Jane Pittman*?

a. Ernest Gaines, Jr.   b. Jane Pittman

c. Harriet Beecher Stowe   d. Jane Austen

You would be wrong to pick "b." It's just too obvious. The correct answer, by the way, is "a."

Second Guessing. Your first impulse, as long as it was based on some sort of reason, is usually correct. Don't go back and change your answers unless you know for sure you were wrong. If it comes down to you saying, "Well, maybe it could be 'A' after all, but I don't know . . . .," stick with your original answer.

Overanalyzing. Sometimes, students see a trick in everything. They try to read between the lines of every question and wind up unable to pick an answer because they think they are falling for a trap. Don't make yourself crazy. Just read the question carefully and accept it at face value.

Misreading. If you skim or read carelessly, you may miss very important words in a question, like *not* or *except*. You might miss the instructions that tell you to "pick all that apply," and wind up giving only one answer when several are required. Stay sharp and pay attention.

THE DREADED SAT (OR ACT)

There is so much hype and so much pressure surrounding the SAT it is no wonder so many students go into high-stress mode about it every year. A little dose of reality would help most students' performance a ton. We are not going to lie and say that your standardized test scores are not important. Most colleges and graduate programs rely on them.

But let's put it into perspective: If you mess up on the test, is your whole family going to be exiled to Siberia? Are you going to be tossed into a pit of snakes? Will the woman you love run off with another man? No, of course not. No one will die. No one will disown you. You might be disappointed. You might have to take the test again and try to do better. At the very worst, you won't get into the college you had your hopes set on. That's a big bummer, but it is something you can live with. Besides, most people who aren't admitted to their number-one college go on to other colleges, graduate, and have perfectly happy, successful lives. So don't approach these tests like a lamb going to the slaughter.

There are many things you can do to maximize your score on the SAT or other standardized admissions tests:

Buy practice tests and take them. The Educational Testing Service, or ETS, designs and administers most of the standardized tests you are familiar with, and many old tests are available at bookstores or through ETS. Take as many as you can, and try to simulate testing conditions—that is, take the test at a desk, and have someone tell you when your time limit is up. The more familiar you are with the structure and content of a test, the better tester you become. A good way to find out more about ETS' tests and services is through their Web site, www.ets.org. You can also phone them at (609) 921-9000.

Buy a prep book. There are dozens of test-preparation books out there that claim to offer score-boosting tips and techniques. Some are useful, and some are not. Pick a book from a company you have heard good things about, preferably a company that also teaches test-preparation courses. That way, you know the tips you are getting have been proven successful by real students. Also, make sure you pick a book that is updated annually, and get the latest copy. The tests do change slightly from year to year, and you need up-to-the minute information. Kaplan's books are an excellent choice. Kaplan offers a complete line of test-prep books designed to suit a variety of needs.

Buy some prep software. If you think that books are old-fashioned, there are all sorts of CD-ROMs and disks out there to help you. Again, look for products from a well-known, reputable company.

Take a prep course. This is the most expensive option (a course can cost several hundred dollars), but it gives the most intensive, hands-on, personal support—provided you pick an experienced, reputable company. Beware of handwritten flyers offering cheap SAT tutoring. You are better off with a proven winner like Kaplan that provides expert instructors and test methods. Call (800) KAP-TEST for more information about courses available near you, or visit kaptest.com on the Web.

At the core of most standardized test preparation is a combination of stress reduction, good time management, and practice—all techniques we have covered in this chapter. Apply these techniques in your schoolwork now, and you will be miles ahead when it comes time for you to face the big exam.

KAPLAN

Chapter 8

In the Library and On the Internet

Odds are, you have been in a library before. You have probably also surfed the Internet. But have you ever had to do some heavy-duty research on an unfamiliar topic in a library so big it makes your high school gym look like an orange crate? Browsing through your local or school library for the latest sci-fi novels or trying to find new games to download off the Net is a lot different from hunting down books and articles on the "the influence of Friedrich Nietzsche's philosophy in Joseph Conrad's *Heart of Darkness*" or "the latest astrophysical techniques for theorizing the presence of black holes in space." You can't just browse around looking for books on these topics and hope to find anything. You have to know how and where to look.

Though libraries, especially major university libraries, can be intimidating in size and the Internet can be intimidating in scope (no one really knows how big it is—spooky, huh?), both can be navigated easily once you master a few key concepts. We will start by focusing on library research, then cover techniques for finding and using Internet documents.

LOOKING STUFF UP IN THE LIBRARY

Luckily, librarians don't keep their books like we keep our CD collection. They wouldn't dream of saying, "Oh, you want a copy of *Moby Dick*? Yeah, I seem to remember it has an orange cover with black writing on it. It's in there somewhere." Librarians actually have a precise system for organizing their holdings and locating items.

Get thee to a library.

Classification Systems

There are two main systems libraries use to code their holdings: the Dewey Decimal System and the Library of Congress system. In both systems, books and other types of materials are labeled with letter/number combinations called "call numbers." Some libraries use both systems simultaneously, labeling some books with Dewey Decimal numbers and some with Library of Congress codes.

The Dewey Decimal System. Used by many smaller libraries, the Dewey Decimal System divides subjects into ten broad areas and assigns a range of numbers, from 0 to 1,000, to those areas. For instance, the numbers 200 to 299 are assigned to "Religion" and the numbers 800–899 are assigned to "Literature." Within each hundred-number block, subjects are broken down further. English drama, for example, gets the number 822.

Of course, there is more than one piece of English drama, so there are further divisions made within each number. After the category number, you will usually see some more letters and numbers—usually the first letter of the author's last name and a few other digits that distinguish one particular title or edition from another. One edition of British writer Oscar Wilde's play *The Importance of Being Earnest*, for example, gets the Dewey Decimal call number 822 W641M.

Books organized using this system are arranged alphanumerically, which means that 821 comes after 820 and so on, and within the 820s, 820 C comes after 820 B. The library shelves are labeled with the numerical range of the books on them, and the spines of the books are clearly marked with their call numbers.

At libraries that use the Dewey Decimal system exclusively, works of fiction and biography are given separate sections. The works of fiction are, sensibly enough, located in a "Fiction" section where they are organized by author's last name. The biographies are marked with "B" and stacked separately.

The Library of Congress System. The Library of Congress system is favored by larger libraries with extensive holdings. It uses letters to break down material into 21 broad areas. The letter "P," for example, is assigned to literature. Each of those broad areas is then narrowed by adding a second letter and/or some numbers. No two books share the same Library of Congress number. In fact, even different editions of the same title get different numbers. In most American books, you can find the Library of Congress number printed on the copyright page. For example, our copy of John Steinbeck's *The Grapes of Wrath* has the call number PS 3537.T3234G8 1986b.

Library shelves will always be clearly marked to show the range of books they contain, and the books will be organized first by letter code (so PS comes after PR) and then by number (so PS 3537 comes after PS 1516).

The Filing System

You don't want to have to memorize two entire classification systems just so you can find a book. Fortunately, you don't have to. That is what the library's filing system is for. It lets you search for books by title, author, subject, and sometimes keyword.

An Ancient Device Called the "Card Catalog." On the main floor of most libraries, you will find cabinets containing small, alphabetized drawers filled with cards. This is the card catalog, and for many decades, this was the filing system all libraries used to help people find what they were looking for. Today, most major libraries use a computerized filing system (more on those in a second), but many local libraries and specialized libraries still use card catalogs, so it is worth familiarizing yourself with how they work.

Each book in the library is represented by up to three different cards: an author card, a title card, and a subject card. All of these cards are filed together. So if you wanted information on, say, leeches, you would look for the "L" drawer and find many different books under the subject heading "leeches." If you knew of a great book on leeches called *Those Amazing Leeches*, you could look in the "T" drawer for that title (note: *a*, *an*, and *the* are left off the beginning of titles for alphabetizing purposes). Or, if you knew only that Cheryl Mays Halton had written a book on leeches, but you didn't know the title, you could look in the "H" drawer for Halton and find the book listed under her name.

Each card for a book contains the call number, the name of the author, the title (obviously), the name and location of the publisher, the publication date, the length of the book, and much more. You can use this information to decide if the book is suitable for you. For example, you may decide that a 20-year-old book on plastic surgery will not have sufficiently up-to-date information in it, and prefer to look for books published within the past five years. If you do decide to check out a book, use a piece of scrap paper to write down the complete call number, the author's last name, and the title.

Posted somewhere in the library will be a guide or map that will tell you which call numbers are stored in which parts of the library. If you can't find this guide or it seems confusing to you, just ask a librarian to point you in the right direction.

Computerized Filing Systems. Computerized filing systems are available at most big libraries. All of them offer the basic functions served by the card catalog: you can search by author, title, or subject to find the call number and publication information for the books you want. The cool thing is, most computerized systems offer much more than the basics. Different libraries use different programs and search commands, but some of the common features you might find are:

- *Keyword searches.* This function help you search for combinations of subjects. Say you were trying to write a paper on the popularity of cricket (the sport, not the insect) in Singapore. Using a card catalog, you would have to search for both "Singapore" and "sports—cricket." With a keyword search, you could combine the terms "Singapore" and "cricket," and complete your search at the touch of a button.

- *Search limitation.* Some systems let you limit the scope of your search by publication date, language, or other factors. Maybe you are researching a paper on Miguel de Cervantes, the Spanish writer, and you are having to wade through all sorts of entries for books written in Spanish. You don't read Spanish. You might be able to limit the search to English-language books and save yourself some time.

- *Book status information.* This saves you the trouble of hunting for a book that has already been checked out. Computerized systems often let you know if the book you want has been checked out, when it is due back, or whether it has been lost, recalled, or sent out for rebinding.

- *Remote access.* If you have a computer and modem, you might be able to access your library's filing system through the Internet. This means you can do a lot of your research from home, late at night, dressed in your Winnie the Pooh jammies. You can arrive at the library with a list of all the books you want already printed out.

- *Electronic renewal.* This is a godsend, especially if you are working on a major research paper over several weeks. In years past, if you wanted to renew your books, you had to cart them all in and have them restamped, then cart them all back home again. It was a major ordeal. With a computerized filing system, you can renew your books from one of the library's computer terminals—or from home, if you have remote access. Say good-bye to library fines.

Read help screens carefully or ask a librarian for help before you start searching. It's easy to get stuck if you don't know the commands that move you around the system.

Looking for Magazine, Journal, and Newspaper Articles

It is always a good idea, especially when researching a paper, to search for magazine, journal, or newspaper articles on your topic of interest. There is a load of information out there that has not made its way into books, and you do not want to miss it.

The Good, Old-Fashioned Printed Index. Ten or 15 years ago, this was your only option. Today, it is still a good option, especially if your school's computer facilities are unreliable or overcrowded. For every major academic area there is an index of periodical literature (that means articles) broken down by subject. These indexes are located in the reference section of your library. Your librarian can help you find the appropriate index for the area you are researching. Some common guides are the *Reader's Guide to Periodical Literature*, *Academic Abstracts*, and *Magazine Index*, *MLA Bibliography*, and *Social Sciences Index*.

You will find yourself confused in a hurry if you just open one of these guides and start flipping through it. Always read the "how to use this guide" section at the front of any index when using it for the first time.

Computerized and Online Indexes. Your library might also offer computerized versions of its periodical indexes. It should come as no surprise that this format is popular with students. From one computer station, students can gain access to several different indexes and do complicated searches quickly and easily. Many libraries also offer students Internet access to these indexes, so they can do some of their research from home or other locations. Another big bonus offered by computerized indexes is that more and more frequently, the full text of the articles indexed are available for downloading, which saves students from having to hunt them down in the library.

Check with the reference librarian if you don't know what kind of computer resources are available to you. And make sure you read the introductory screen and help sections your index makes available before starting your search.

You Found an Article That Looks Interesting. Now what? While searching through your index, you found an article that looks like it may be very helpful to you. If the text of that article is not available online, you will need to find it in your library. To do this, you should write down the name of the article, the name of the author, the magazine or journal in which it appeared, the volume/issue number or date, and the page number on which the article appears. "Volume" refers to a set—often a year's worth—of magazine issues. If a magazine started publishing monthly issues in 1970, for example, the April, 1975, issue might called volume 6 (because the magazine is in its sixth year of publication), number 4 (because the April issue is the fourth issue of that volume). Here is an example of an entry we found on a computerized index:

> Vidal, Gore/"Twain on the Grand Tour: Mark Twain's Trips Around the World."/New York Review of Books: May 23, 1996, v43, n9, p25/4 pages

From this entry, we can tell the author's last name is Vidal, his first name is Gore, and the title of the article is "Twain on the Grand Tour . . . ." The article was published in the *New York Review of Books* on May 23, 1996. The volume number is 43, the issue number is 9, and the article appears on page 25.

When you have the information noted, you will need to look up the name of the magazine or journal in your library's filing system as if it were a book. The listing will tell you where to look for the issue of the magazine you want. It may be stored in the stacks, in the periodical section, or on microfilm or microfiche. Read on to find out more about locating sources in different formats.

WHERE IS EVERYTHING?

Every library has a different layout, but most share the same basic sections. Here's the general breakdown:

The Stacks. This term refers to what's usually the largest part of the library— the place where most of the books are "stacked" (get it?) on the shelves. Within the stacks, there is an "oversized" section for books too large or long to fit on the regular shelves. If the book you are looking for is oversized, it will be noted on listing in the filing system.

The Reference Section. Encyclopedias, almanacs, indexes to periodical literature, dictionaries, statistical reports, and all sorts of other general informational material are separated from the rest of the books into their own section. Facts, facts, and more facts are what you will find here. It is a great place to get your feet wet when starting a project on an unfamiliar topic.

The Periodical Section. Newer issues of magazines and newspapers are stored alphabetically by title on racks or shelves in the periodical section.

Microfilm and Microfiche. Microfilm and microfiche are inexpensive methods for storing large amounts of printed material in a small space. Old issues of newspapers and magazines are often kept in these formats. In the microfilm/microfiche area, you will find cabinets with alphabetized drawers filled with boxes organized by publication name and date.

You must use a special viewing machine to read your issue. If you have never used these formats before, don't make yourself nuts. If you can't figure out how to load and run the machines, ask a librarian.

Audiovisual Section. This section holds films, videotapes, and sound recordings that are especially helpful for students in areas like anthropology, archeology, art, and music.

Special Collections. Many libraries have collections of rare books, very old books, letters, diaries, and other material that they keep separate from the rest of their resources. Access to these documents is often restricted and you are usually not allowed to take them out of the library. See your special collections librarian for details.

LOOKING STUFF UP ON THE INTERNET

The danger with putting advice in a book about how to search the Internet is that by the time this book gets printed and reaches you, there will probably be newer and better ways of finding information online—ways that did not exist when we wrote this. The world of computer-assisted communication is changing so rapidly and so drastically, there is no way for us to predict what kinds of powerful tools will be available to you a year or two from now or how they might help you do better in school. Nevertheless, we are going to take our chances and give you some general pointers and guidelines for using electronic sources.

World Wide Web Search Engines

When the World Wide Web first emerged in the early 1990s, people were excited. The Internet had been used to transfer files and e-mail messages for years, but the Web brought full-color photos and sound together on hyperlinked documents. It was, and still is, very cool. The problem at first, however, was that you could only look at one of these Web "pages" if you knew the exact uniform resource locator address, or URL (that thing that usually begins with "www"). There was no way to browse around for sites that might be of interest to you. In an effort to address this problem, several publishers put together Internet "phone books" that worked kind of like yellow pages, with sites grouped by category. The drawback was that new sites kept springing up and old sites kept disappearing faster than any publisher could keep up. And quite honestly, the contents of the early Web sites were of little interest to students doing academic research.

The solution to the problem of finding documents was the development of search engines. Search engines allow Web users to use keywords and search commands to find the information they want. Some of the more popular search engines, with their Internet addresses, are:

AltaVista—www.altavista.com

Excite!—www.excite.com

Google—www.google.com

Lycos—www.lycos.com

Yahoo!—www.yahoo.com

The content issue has sort of taken care of itself. As the Web has grown in popularity, countless exciting, useful Web sites have been developed. You will find authoritative Web pages devoted to almost any topic you can think of.

We are going to assume you know the basics of getting around on the Web, like how to scroll through a document, how to follow hyperlinks, how to use URLs, and how to move back and forth between pages. If you don't, any introductory guide to the Web (available at bookstores and your library) will get you up to speed.

Every search engine works slightly differently. Before you begin, read through all the help sections for guidelines. In general, all you have to do is type in a few words that you think would appear in a document you want to read. For example, if you wanted to research the history of the ancient stone structure known as Stonehenge and its possible use by Druid priests in rituals of human sacrifice (what a gory topic you picked!), you might start by searching for:

Stonehenge Druids sacrifice

Searching for Stonehenge

The trouble is, if you simply enter these three words, your search engine will look for every document that contains any of these words. We tried it, and the search engine presented us with over 12,000 documents to look at. A bit overwhelming.

To narrow your search, most search engines let you use "+" to mark words that must appear in your search and "–" to mark words that must not appear in your search. So if we are interested only in documents that talk about Stonehenge, Druids, and human sacrifice, all in the same document, and we are not interested in any documents about Stonehenge's possible astronomical uses, we might try searching this way:

+Stonehenge +Druids +sacrifice –astronomical

This search turned up just over a hundred documents for us, including an interesting article from Britannia Online at www.britannia.com/wonder/michell2.html. Check it out, if you are curious.

If your first search attempts turn up nothing of interest, don't give up. Try thinking of more words that absolutely must turn up in your document, and add them to your search. Practice is the best (and most fun) way to get the hang of this.

Other E-Sources

The World Wide Web isn't the only Internet game in town. There are some other e-sources out there that can help you in your quest for information.

Newsgroups. There are thousands of Internet newsgroups organized around thousands of different interests. Newsgroups work kind of like electronic bulletin boards. A user with a question or comment posts it for the rest of the group to read, then interested group members post their responses. Major Web browsing programs like Netscape Navigator and Microsoft's Internet Explorer offer newsgroup functions that let you check out a list of available newsgroups and participate in discussions.

Newsgroups can be very useful for tracking down obscure information. They can also be big wastes of time in which people with nothing better to do vent their emotions at others. Choose the group you join carefully.

E-mail and listservs. It seems like everyone has an e-mail address these days. That can work to your advantage if you are hunting for information. Many Web reference sites include e-mail addresses and encourage comments and questions. If you have the time to wait patiently for a response, you will find most of these organizations very helpful.

A listserv is an e-mailing list organized around a particular area of interest. Articles are posted, ideas are shared, arguments are waged. As with a mailing list, you must subscribe. And listservs, unlike newsgroups, are often monitored, so you rarely see bizarre, offensive postings. Ask friends or professors about any listservs they belong to. You might be interested in joining yourself. It is a great way to keep up with the latest developments in a field.

Evaluate Your Sources Carefully!

You have heard the old warning, "Don't believe everything you read." This goes double for documents on the Internet. With traditional sources like books and magazines, you can be reasonably sure that the material you are looking at has been created, reviewed, and evaluated by people who are authorities in their areas. A person who wanted to write a book about Nazis, for example, would be unlikely to find a reputable publisher unless she could show that she had the necessary education, background, and writing skills to create such a book. Notice we said a "reputable" publisher. There will always be unscrupulous magazine and book publishers who try to forward their own agendas with lies and slanted material. Since books and magazines have been around for centuries, most people have gotten pretty good at evaluating these sources and separating the good from the bad.

The trouble with the Internet is that it is sometimes hard to tell the "reputable," reliable sources from the "unscrupulous," biased ones. You don't want to make a jerk of yourself by quoting statistics from the Web site of some cleverly disguised hate group, so before you rely on any information you find online, ask yourself the following questions:

1. What organization or person created the information I am looking at? Look at the URL for clues. Certain suffixes appear in the addresses of different types of organizations. For example, a Web site address with ".com" means that the company running the site is a commercial organization. An address with ".org" usually means the organization is not-for-profit (that doesn't mean, however, that the organization doesn't have a specific agenda). The suffix ".gov" marks government sites, which are good sources of reliable statistical information. The suffix ".edu" marks educational sites, like university Web pages. These are most often reliable sources.

2. Is there a strong religious or political bias in this material? If so, you may want to take any statistics or "facts" quoted with a grain of salt, or try to substantiate them through other sources.

3. What credentials does the author have? If you can't find out anything about the author of an Internet document, you might not want to rely on it. Any academic research you do should be based on authoritative sources, like articles by professional, journalists, professors, or people with first-hand knowledge of a topic. A Web site on Somalian politics by someone you can identify only as "Joey from Toledo, Ohio" is not likely to be the reputable source you are looking for.

There are no publishers or editors out there evaluating *all* the material that winds up on the Internet. That means you have to be much more critical of what you read online than what you read offline. A touch of skepticism will go a long way.

Chapter 9

Paper Writing the Painless Way

There are few things more daunting than a blank page or empty computer screen staring you in the face, daring you to write something. If the thought of starting a paper leaves you numb, you are not alone. Would it surprise you that the vast majority of students rate writing as one of their weakest skills? Many businessmen and businesswomen feel the same way. There is just something about putting your thoughts on paper that makes you feel vulnerable.

Starting a writing project is never easy, even for professional writers. But don't sell yourself short. Okay, so you may not be the next winner of a Nobel Prize for literature. Join the club. You can, however, learn to write clear, organized, interesting papers that earn good grades. All it takes is a little planning and a little confidence.

Just one note before we get started. You will be assigned many different kinds of papers throughout high school. You may be asked to take a position on a controversial issue and argue your point of view in an essay. You may be asked to summarize a body of work in a report. You may be asked to do independent research on a topic and write a long paper about it. This chapter lays out a framework for approaching long research papers. The steps we include will help no matter what kind of writing assignment you have, but some steps apply more to certain types of papers than to others. Tailor our advice to suit your needs, and omit steps that obviously don't apply to your writing assignment.

Don't Touch That Keyboard Yet!

When you have a tough task ahead of you, you may have the temptation to just sit right down, do it, and get it over with. That is a wonderful impulse, but when you are approaching a paper, you should not plunge into writing straight off. That would be like charging into the jungle without so much as a compass and a machete. Ever heard the old saying, "An ounce of prevention is worth a pound of cure"? When applied to writing, it means that coming up with an interesting, suitable topic and doing a little preliminary research to refine it *before you start writing* will save you from hours of frustration later when you discover your paper is not working out. Channel that urge to get going into the planning stage of your paper.

Selecting a Topic

Your instructor may give you anything from a very specific to a very general topic, but you will always have some leeway as to how you want to approach it. There are only two rules to follow when picking an approach or topic: Make it something you find interesting, and make it feasible.

Making It Interesting. Following both of these rules is a little trickier than it may seem. Let's face it, you are required to take a lot of courses you don't find completely engaging. A topic related to the class that also interests you might not immediately spring to mind. If you find yourself uninspired by a class you are taking and unable to come up with a paper idea, try thinking of the assignment in terms of something you do like. For example, let's say you are taking a history class and studying the European Renaissance. Your instructor wants you to write a paper on the French Enlightenment (the Enlightenment was an intellectual movement of the seventeenth and eighteenth centuries that focused on the powers of the human mind and science). You are not really a history fan, but you are interested in fashion and interior design. You could write a paper on the effects Enlightenment ideas had on fashion and interior design in France. Or maybe you are a budding mathematician. If so, you might want to write a paper on the influence of René Descartes, a famous seventeenth-century French mathematician and philosopher.

Get the idea? You can't stray from the assigned topic (obviously, in the example above you would have to learn quite a bit about the French Enlightenment no matter what), but you can approach it in a way that you find exciting. This way, your research seems less like a chore and more like an exploration of one of your interests. And your teacher will appreciate your fresh perspective on the topic.

Making It Feasible. Interesting, however, is not enough. You actually have to be able to follow through and do a thorough job in the allotted time. This is where the question of feasibility comes in. Does your library have the resources you need to pursue the topic that interests you? Is the information you require available free of charge, or will you have to pay for it? Does your topic require a lot of background research in an area you have no familiarity with? Will you have time to do that research? You have many responsibilities and other school assignments. There is only so much time you can devote to any one project. Challenge yourself, but don't bite off more than you can chew.

> ## *Note to Self*
>
> *Pass It By Your Teacher*
>
> Once you have come up with an idea for your paper, it can be very helpful to talk to your instructor about it. It is a fast, easy way to clear up any misunderstandings about the assignment before you do a lot of work. Also, your instructor can give you some helpful guidance about how to proceed with your topic: the names of books to check out, articles to read, experts to consult. This can save you some library time.

Too Narrow or Too Broad? When it comes to settling on a topic, which is better: narrow or broad? Neither. Your topic must be exactly suited to the length of your assigned paper. Not so broad that you can't treat it in detail, and not so narrow that you run out of things to say, repeat yourself, or beat your point to death.

The problem most students have is topics that are too broad. For example, let's say you were assigned a five-page paper in your American literature class. Your instructor gave you the general topic: the fiction of Nathaniel Hawthorne. You decide to write your paper on "Hawthorne's interpretation of Puritan theology as seen in his short stories." Is this topic too narrow or too broad?

Too broad. Hawthorne wrote many short stories, quite a few of which dealt with Puritan theology. It would take a book-length paper to cover this topic in sufficient detail. You could narrow the topic by picking only one aspect of Puritan theology—maybe the doctrine of predestination—and apply it to one or two stories. Or you could select one story and analyze its use of a few different aspects of Puritan theology.

Many students are amazed at how much information and argumentation it takes to prove a point or cover a topic. The more you write, the better feel you will develop for how much is enough. See the "Try This" below for a little more practice. And if you find yourself in doubt about a topic, ask your instructor.

Try This

Decide whether the following topics are too narrow or too broad, then try to adjust each one so it fits the length requirement.

1. A 15-page paper about "World War I."
2. A three-page paper about "the paintings of Pablo Picasso."
3. A five-page paper about "how to boil an egg."
4. A 15-page paper explaining "why Han Solo is cooler than Luke Skywalker."
5. A ten-page paper on "various theories about the structure of atoms."

Once you have a suitably adjusted, interesting, feasible topic, it's time to hit the library to take it for a test drive.

Preliminary Research and Refinement

Chapter eight contains all the information you need about looking up and locating books, articles, Web pages, and other materials. Make sure to read it, even if you consider yourself a library pro. There is plenty of helpful, time-saving information there. What we are going to focus on here is what to do with the books and articles once you have them.

Preliminary Research. What we mean by "preliminary research" is a quick-and-dirty library trip designed to make sure that your topic is on target. It shouldn't take you long to figure this out. Go to the library and find three or four books that address your topic in a broad way. The encyclopedias in your library's reference section are a great place to start. Skim through them, lingering on parts that you find interesting. Try to identify the major issues involved with your topic, and see if there are opposing viewpoints.

Most researchers have an idea in their head of what they will discover before they even begin their preliminary research. How can this be, you ask? Isn't the point of doing research to find answers, not to decide what the answer will be ahead of time? Yes and no. It helps to have some idea of what you are looking for before you start reading, otherwise it is difficult to find a good place to dive in. Your preconceived belief gives you a jumping off point.

However, you must be flexible and open-minded enough to change your position on a topic if necessary. Don't just see what you want to see and use only the facts and opinions that support your original idea. Be willing to admit you could be mistaken.

Refining Your Idea. During or after your preliminary research trip, you may find yourself more excited about the topic than ever. It may turn out that the topic is far richer than you imagined. You may find that you changed your mind about some important point or that you held some mistaken assumptions. You may even decide to toss out your original idea in favor of a completely new one.

All of these are fine options. This is what preliminary research is for. It is kind of like premarital counseling. You do not want to commit to your topic and start writing only to discover later that you have irreconcilable differences. By then, it will be too late for a divorce. Reevaluate your idea based on its interest to you and its feasibility. Do you still like your idea? Do you think there is enough information on the topic for you to write a paper? If not, tweak your topic.

NOTETAKING AND ORGANIZATION

Now you have a refined, exciting topic and you have done enough preliminary research to have at least some clue as to what the major points of your paper will be. Before you go any further, you need a game plan. In this case, that means a preliminary outline and a notetaking system.

Preliminary Outline

Block out your paper in a broad outline. To do this, you need to think about what kind of organization would work best for your topic. Do you want to cover an issue in chronological order? Do you have a few main issues to discuss? If so, in what order should you discuss them? Do you need to explain or define certain concepts or lay any groundwork before you can begin to make your main points?

You have many options when organizing your paper. Any structure is fine, as long as the ideas flow logically. Here's an example of what your preliminary outline might look like if you were writing a paper about the influence Henry David Thoreau's essay "On Civil Disobedience" had on Mahatma Gandhi and Dr. Martin Luther King Jr.:

Sample: Preliminary Outline

I. Introduction—An assertion that Thoreau's work, and "On Civil Disobedience" in particular, has been important in many struggles for freedom and justice around the world. Two notable examples: the struggles led by Gandhi and King.

II. Background on Thoreau and "On Civil Disobedience"

    A. Details of Thoreau's life and major works

    B. Summary and analysis of "On Civil Disobedience"

    C. Info about how Thoreau's essay was received at the time

III. Gandhi and the struggle for Indian independence

    A. Background on the struggle in India in the first decades of the 20th century

    B. Background on Gandhi, his education, his interpretation of Thoreau

    C. Details of Gandhi's civil disobedience efforts in India

IV. Dr. Martin Luther King Jr. and equal rights

    A. Background on racism in the United States in the 1940s, '50s, and '60s

    B. Background on King, his education, his interpretation of Thoreau

    C. Details of King's leadership and civil disobedience.

  V. Conclusion—Mention sit-ins and other nonviolent protests that have sprung from Thoreau's writing, and note the impressive, important results of civil disobedience in India and the United States.

This outline reveals several considerations. First, since you will be discussing the influence of one person on two others, it makes sense to discuss that person first, so your readers will have the background they need to understand the comparisons you will make. Secondly, it is logical to treat the two main subjects of your paper—Gandhi and King—in separate sections. Thirdly, Gandhi is placed before King because the struggle for independence in India occurred before King began his Civil Rights movement. Notice the introduction offers a general statement that sets the stage for the paper and the conclusion echoes but does not repeat the introduction.

Remember, this is your preliminary outline. You will have to give it much more detail before you start to write, you will probably have to change it a bit, and you may even have to reorganize it dramatically. Now, with your outline in hand, go to the library and hunt down material on all the various points you need to cover.

Making a Statement

Before you continue, ask yourself what your paper is about, then write down your answer in one sentence (it can be a long sentence). This sentence is your thesis statement. Writing teachers often tell students to use their thesis statements to start their papers, but this is not necessary. Your thesis can be implied or stated in several sentences. The real reason you need to come up with a thesis statement is that it forces you to focus precisely on what it is you are trying to say or prove. If you find it difficult to write one sentence that sums up the point of your paper, your readers will also have a tough time figuring out what your point is.

Did You Know...

Digging Deeper with Bibliographies

During your preliminary research, you gathered some general materials on your topic. If, after searching every way you can, you are still coming up short on materials, try flipping to the back of the books you have checked out and reading through their bibliographies and source lists. Often, bibliographies will hold the names of many interesting articles and books listed that don't turn up during subject or keyword searches.

Taking Note: It's All in the Cards

When it comes time to plow through that huge pile of material in front of you, you will need to have a note-taking system planned. Of course, you can feel free to come up with your own system if you want, but why make things tough on yourself? Profit from the toil of the countless students who came before you and perfected the "index card system."

This is our favorite system. It works just as well for three-page papers as it does for 100-page papers. It is flexible. It is easy. It gives you the courage to face that blank page bravely. Here's how it works:

First, get yourself several packets of index cards—big ones if you write big, little ones if you write small. Take out one card for every piece of material you have, and write a bibliographic listing for each piece, one listing per card. Use whatever guidelines your instructor has given you for this, or refer to the *MLA Handbook* (your library will have a copy) for rules. When you are done, organize the cards according to author/editor's last name. In the upper right-hand corner, mark each card with a letter: A, B, C, D, and so on. If you have more than 26 sources, start again with AA, BB, etcetera.

Here is an example:

M

Turkle, Sherry. Life on the Screen: Identity in the Age of the Internet.

New York: Simon & Schuster, 1995.

KAPLAN

Begin reading through your material. When you find a fact you want to make note of, take out a card and write the information down on one side of the card. If everything won't fit on one side of one card, use two different cards. In the upper right-hand corner of the card, write the letter that corresponds to the source you are using and the page number the information comes from.

Here is an example:

M, p. 85

"For more than three decades, from the early 1950s to the mid-1980s, the Turing test, named after the British mathematician Alan Turing who first proposed it, was widely accepted as a model for thinking about the line between machines and people."

When you are finished with your research, spread your cards out on your desk or on the floor and consider them in terms of your outline. Use your cards to create a new, very detailed outline, and organize your cards to follow along with it.

With this system, there will be no desperate, last-minute searching through articles for that perfect quote or statistic you "lost." No precariously balanced pile of books next to your computer. Just a nice, neat stack of cards. Writing your paper becomes a matter of "hooking" your cards together. The letters and page numbers in the corners of your cards make crediting your sources simple, and your source cards make writing your bibliography a breeze.

IT'S FINALLY TIME TO WRITE YOUR FIRST DRAFT

There are really only two keys to learning to write well: practicing and reading a wide variety of excellent writing. Practicing, of course, makes anything better. Reading great writing—and that can mean anything from great works of literature to great greeting cards—helps you develop an ear for what works.

Keep writing and keep reading. You'll see.

There are, of course, some practical tips we can give you right now to help you get through your next paper successfully:

Block Out a Big Chunk Of Time

Ever notice that if you sit down to read a book and put it down after reading only five or ten pages, you often never pick it up again? Or if you do pick it up, you have to reread the same five or ten pages? You have to start over because you didn't give yourself time to get into it—to identify the main plot lines and characters.

The same is true for writing. It takes some time to get into the rhythm. We suggest blocking out at least two hours when starting your paper (that is, as long as the paper is supposed to be three pages long or longer). Two hours is roughly long enough for you stare at the screen or page for a while, wrestle with a few ideas, and finally hammer out about three pages. That's a good start. You are at least past your introduction and into the body of the paper. When you return to the paper, you will be able to pick up your train of thought and continue. You have established a rhythm. Don't let yourself stop until you have three pages.

Don't Edit as You Go

Writing your first draft is all about "flow." Once you get into that rhythm, don't agonize over your grammar or spelling, and don't stop to nit-pick your writing. There is time for that later, when you are proofreading. Just get those ideas into writing. Keep them coming!

KAPLAN

Make Sure to Follow Your Teacher's Guidelines

If your teacher gave you a style sheet or formatting guidelines, follow his instructions exactly. Put page numbers where he says, list your sources the way he wants. And whatever you do, don't try to get cute with font sizes, line spacing, and margins, hoping to fool your instructor into thinking your paper is longer than it really is. Your instructor knows very well what a properly formatted paper looks like, and you will only hurt your grade by using giant type and triple spacing.

Your instructor might refer you to a style handbook for formatting and citation guidelines (we'll explain more about "citations" in just a minute). The most common style handbooks are those published by the Modern Language Association (MLA) and the American Psychological Association (APA). The MLA puts out the *MLA Handbook for Writers of Research Papers* and the *MLA Style Manual*. Both contain details on MLA style and citation method, which are used for papers in the arts and humanities (fine arts, history, literature, etcetera). The APA puts out a book called the *Publication Manual of the American Psychological Association*. APA style and citation methods are used for scientific papers. You can find both in your library.

Cite Your Sources

Citing your sources is just a way of giving credit where credit is due. It means letting your reader know the source of any quotes, figures, or ideas you did not personally come up with. If you take someone else's published words or interpretations and use them without giving credit, you are stealing. This kind of stealing is called plagiarism, and it is a very serious offense that can earn you an F on your paper and maybe even get you expelled.

When you are struggling with a difficult paper, it can seem awfully tempting to just let a few citations slide and use another writer's words to make yourself look better. After all, you may tell yourself, how will your instructor ever find out? You'd be surprised. Remember, your

> ### *Note to Self*
>
> *Invest in a Good Grammar and Style Handbook*
>
> You will probably have to write many papers, reports, proposals, memos, and other documents in your life. And no matter how often you brush up, there will always be those little grammatical points you can never quite remember (is it *that* or *which*? *Lay* or *lie*? *Who* or *whom*?). A good, thorough grammar and style book is a handy desk reference.

instructor is an expert in the field she teaches. She has probably read most of the books and articles you used for your paper. She is much more familiar with your topic than you might imagine. And she is probably an experienced writer who has a knack for detecting the slight variations in tone and style that signal the presence of another person's "voice" in your paper. Plagiarism makes teachers furious. Even if she only suspects you cheated, believe us, your teacher will make it her business to find out for sure. Don't risk the consequences.

It can be hard to figure out what to cite and what not to, but it gets easier with practice. Here are just a couple of things to bear in mind:

1. You don't have to cite historical or scientific facts—only interpretations of those facts.

2. Even if you paraphrase a quote, if you are using someone else's idea, you have to cite the source.

Tell It Like a Story

Finding the right style and tone for a paper can be a struggle. Many students go overboard in their attempts to write in formal, academic language and their papers wind up being both confusing and stuffy. Their impulse is correct, though. The kind of writing you use for a research paper should be more formal than the kind of writing you use when writing a letter to a close friend. But you can still keep your own voice and style.

Try writing your paper as if you were narrating an interesting story for an important foreign diplomat to listen to. The diplomat speaks very good, precise English, but cannot follow long sentences or understand slang expressions and contractions. You want to speak naturally, respectfully, and clearly. That way, your story will not be bogged down by cumbersome sentences or tarnished by trendy catchphrases and clichés.

Did You Know...

Online Sources

As more and more information finds its way onto the Internet, you will be increasingly likely to use online sources in your papers. The *MLA Handbook* does offer guidelines for citing some types of Internet sources (like Web pages), but new types of electronic documents keep springing up faster than the authorities can makes rules about them. This doesn't let you off the "citation" hook, though. If you can't find specific guidelines for the type of document you are using, adapt accepted guidelines as best you can.

EDITING, REVISING, AND PROOFREADING

After you finish your first draft, if time permits, leave it alone for a couple of days. Don't look at it or think about it. You need some time for your brain to settle down so you can look at your paper with a fresh perspective. At the very least, give yourself eight hours, sleeping or awake.

When you feel refreshed, pick up your rough draft and a colored pen (blue or red is fine) and read your paper critically, as if it were someone else's paper and you were grading it. Try to find mistakes, rough patches, or places where there seem to be gaps in your reasoning. Every error you find and correct is one your instructor won't have to mark. It can help a great deal to read your draft aloud. If you find yourself stumbling over a sentence, that is a good indication that the sentence is awkwardly worded and needs to be rephrased. If you find yourself confused by your paper, you know for sure your reader will be, too.

Be on especially sharp lookout for:

- *Very long paragraphs.* A paragraph should contain a block of related information. Using paragraphs well helps guide your reader and break up your ideas into digestible pieces. Paragraphs that run for more than a page can leave your reader feeling lost.

- *Very long sentences.* The longer your sentence, the more likely it is you will make a grammatical goof. Plus, your reader will have a hard time following you.

- *Run-ons, fragments, and other grammatical errors.* Run-ons (two or more sentences jammed together without a proper link) and fragments (incomplete sentences) plague high school papers. Reading your paper out loud will help you identify these mistakes.

To help you with the proofreading stage, we've included a checklist of writing trouble spots at the end of this chapter. Using a checklist will help you to proofread your paper systematically.

Once you have edited your paper, go back and address all the problems you noted.

You now have a second draft. If you are composing on a computer, use the spell-checker at this point. But be aware that a spell-checker will not catch all spelling errors. If you typed *there* instead of *their* or *tow* instead of *two*, the mistake will remain. Read through your paper once more as carefully as possible, looking for spelling errors—or better yet, have someone whose spelling and grammar skills are good read through your paper for you. Fix any typos and check one more time to make sure that your paper satisfies your teacher's guidelines.

After that, you're done! Pat yourself on the back, kick back, and relax.

PROOFREADING CHECKLIST

This proofreading checklist will help you to proofread your papers, essays, and homework assignments methodically. You'll notice that each of the categories contains extra blank spaces. You can use these spaces to jot down any errors you're particularly prone to make. Feel free to photocopy this checklist and use it on all your writing.

Paragraph Structure

❑ **Very Long Paragraphs:** Make sure that each paragraph contains a block of related information. Check for paragraphs that run for an entire page or more.

❑ _____

_____

❑ _____

_____

Grammar

❑ **Sentence Fragments:** Make sure that each sentence expresses a complete thought.

❑ **Run-Ons:** Check for sentences that should be broken down into smaller sentences.

❑ **Subject-Verb Agreement:** Make sure singular subjects have singular verbs and plural subjects have plural verbs.

❑ **Pronoun-Noun Agreement:** Check to see that pronouns agree with the nouns they replace.

❑ _____

_____

❑ _____

_____

Usage

❑ **Verb Tense:** Make sure you have used the correct past tense forms of irregular verbs, particularly tricky verbs such as *lie* and *lay*.

❑ _____

_____

❑ _____

_____

Punctuation

❏ **End Punctuation:** Check that each sentence ends with a period, exclamation point, or question mark, depending on what type of sentence it is.

❏ _____

_____

❏ _____

_____

Spelling

❏ **Right Spelling, Wrong Meaning:** Watch out for words that sound alike but have different meanings, such as _fair/fare_, _to/two/too_, and _their/there/they're_. Make sure you've got the right spelling.

❏ **Common Misspellings:** Look out for common spelling errors, such as confusing _ie/ei_ in _friend/receive_, or _cede/ceed_ as in _recede/succeed_, etcetera.

❏ _____

_____

❏ _____

_____

Capitalization

❏ **Proper Nouns:** Check that all proper nouns are capitalized.

❏ **Sentences:** Check that each sentence and each direct quote that is a sentence begins with a capital letter.

❏ _____

_____

❏ _____

_____

Other Things to Watch Out For

❏ _____

_____

❏ _____

_____

Section 3

Troubleshooting

Chapter 10

When Things Go Wrong

The eighteenth-century Scottish poet Robert Burns hit the nail on the head when he wrote, "The best laid schemes o' mice and men/Gang aft a-gley," which basically translates into "no matter how careful you are, sometimes things get messed up." If your life is perfect, good for you. If you are like the rest of us, however, you sometimes make mistakes, get sick, or have personal problems. Sometimes a too-good-to-be-true opportunity even presents itself that makes you throw caution (and your notebook) to the wind—like someone giving you a courtside ticket to an NCAA basketball championship game taking place two states away the day before your midterm.

There are two kinds of situations that can send you reeling off course: situations that aren't your fault, like serious illnesses and family emergencies, and situations that are your fault, like falling behind in all your classes because you stayed an extra two weeks in Cancun after spring break hanging out on the beach with Miguel, the new man of your dreams. What we are about to offer is some advice for salvaging your grades in both types of situations.

Sometimes you'll find yourself WAY OFF COURSE!

Your success in getting back on track will depend on your willingness to work hard and your teacher's willingness to help you.

Let's start with the serious problems.

ILLNESS AND FAMILY EMERGENCIES

Your own illness or an illness or death in your family will always be an understandable, excusable reason for falling behind at school. In order to smooth the way for your return to classes, there are some details you need to take care of when faced with a sickness or personal tragedy.

Your Own Illness. If you can, notify all your instructors individually as soon as you know that you will be missing class. Depending on what type of illness you have, you may be able to study and do schoolwork at home, and your instructors can make arrangements to get assignments to you. This will make catching up later much easier.

If you are too ill to contact all of your instructors individually, you or your parents should call the principal's office and ask someone there to notify your instructors.

An Illness or Death in the Family. It is an unfortunate, disturbing fact that students sometimes pretend a family member is ill or has died in order to get themselves out of a jam at school. "Grandmothers" expire with alarming frequency, and some instructors have become suspicious of students who, a week after missing a test, claim that they had to go to a funeral. This kind of lying puts the instructor in the painful, awkward position of having to question students who truly have suffered tragedies and need sympathy.

If your teacher knows you and trusts you, you will certainly have her immediate support in the event of an illness or death in your family. If you are one of hundreds of students in a large class and your instructor does not know you personally, she may require some sort of back-up. A telephone call or note from a parent or family member will be sufficient.

When an emergency strikes, clearly, your first impulse is not to track down all your instructors and tell them about it. Ask friends to inform your instructors of the situation and give an estimate as to when you might return to school.

When You Return to Class. First, make sure your teacher was notified about the reason for your absence, then make an appointment to speak with him about how you can catch up. If your class has a cumulative final exam, your teacher may disregard any missed work and count that exam for the bulk of your grade. He may allow you to take a make-up test or write a paper in place of a test.

No matter what, you will have to work extra hard for a while to master all the material you missed while you were gone. That can be very tough, especially if you are still feeling weak or depressed. Here are some hints to get you over the hump:

- Ask for help from your teacher and from friends. They will be happy to assist you.

- Don't be too hard on yourself. Recognize that after an emotional or physical ordeal, you might not be at the top of your form. Your grades might slip a bit. That is okay. Just do the best you can.

- Be proud of yourself for hanging in there. Even if your grades do slip, you are showing a lot of strength and commitment by trying to keep up.

- Cut out any nonessential duties. If it is at all possible, let go of any part-time jobs or obligations. You need to cut down on the amount of pressure in your life. Once you get back up to speed, you can start taking on more responsibilities again.

Should You Withdraw from School? Pulling out of school for a while after something bad happens can seem like a great option, but we do not recommend it. It leaves you behind your friends and classmates and delays your graduation. Some students find it very hard to get back into the school habit after a long break and wind up dropping out for good.

YOU GOOFED OFF AND FELL BEHIND

You have been cutting class because you were busy surfing/spending time with your new girlfriend/sleeping/playing games involving pocket change and glasses of beer. You haven't done any reading because you were too involved in your social activities/unaware that the class had a textbook/lazy/obsessed with global warming. If only these were legitimate excuses, a much smaller percentage of high school students would fail each semester. If it has suddenly dawned on you that you are in big, big trouble at school—that is, you have a test or paper due in a couple of days and you haven't begun to prepare—take heart: You may yet be able to save your skin.

None of the techniques we are about to cover is an effective substitute for good, consistent study habits. In fact, none of these techniques will guarantee you a good grade. What we are shooting for here is a *passing* grade.

It Can't Hurt to Turn Over a New Leaf

Mind Boost

Aren't We Contradicting Ourselves?

A lot of the advice we are giving here contradicts what we say in early chapters. That is because our early chapters are about earning good grades while actually learning the material covered in your classes. The advice we are giving here is about minimizing the damage to your GPA once you've already made mistakes.

If you really believe in your heart that your days of slacking off are over and you now plan to be a model student, it can be worthwhile to set up an appointment with your instructor, admit that you have been goofing off, ask for advice about getting back on track, and declare that you will sin no more. Only do this if you truly mean it. You don't want to look like a phony. But even if you are sincere, don't expect too much sympathy from your instructor. Remember, your actions speak louder than your words, and a quick apology will not wipe away a history of sloppy homework and skipped classes.

Your heart-to-heart may not help you at all, but it's worth a shot. You just want your instructor to give you the benefit of the doubt one more time. So do what you must to make good on your promise to do better. And whatever you do, don't skip class the day after your meeting.

Desperate Measures for Desperate Times

It's only one or two days before the big test or the big due date, and you have not been studying for weeks. This situation demands two things above all: calm and focus. Now is not the time to lose your nerve. Put yourself "in the zone" and stay confident and relaxed.

Cramming. The trouble with cramming for a test is that you are not really learning anything. Most of what you stuff into your brain will disappear within a few hours or days. But if all you are after is a passing grade, you may manage to retain enough information in your short term memory to do the trick.

Step One: Call a friend or classmate. Make sure you know what format the test will be in (open book, multiple choice, essay, etcetera). If she will let you, photocopy your friend's notes. If she tells you to find someone else to mooch from, accept her judgment gracefully.

Step Two: Use your textbook to create a master study outline, then fill it in with your newly acquired notes. To do this, assess your time limit first. Are you going to have to cover a whole semester in one night? If so, you will only be able to skim through the text. Focus on headings, chapter summaries, highlighted words, the first and last sentences of every paragraph, formulas, and definitions. If you have less to cover, you can read a little more carefully. On some notebook paper, create an outline of the chapters as you read. When you have finished reading, review the notes you borrowed. This will give you some idea of what your instructor stressed in class. Try to fit details from the notes into your outline. If you are studying for a literature exam, read as many of the short pieces as you can in their entirety, and look for summaries of longer pieces. If you are studying for a math exam, try to do at least five sample problems from every chapter in your textbook.

Step Three: Make some "must-know" flashcards. You won't be able to memorize every term in your book in one night, so pick the 20 or so of the most important definitions or formulas and focus on them.

Step Four: Read your outline and flip through your flashcards over and over until you are too tired to continue. Then stop. Sleep for at least four hours. Set your alarm so that you have an hour before the test starts to read your outline and flip through your flashcards some more.

Step Five: Keep reading that outline and flipping through those cards until the moment the bell rings and your instructor tells you to put your notes away.

On Your Essay Test. Read through the test, pick the questions you feel most capable of answering (if you are given an option), and figure out about how much time you can afford to spend on each question. Then quickly write down anything you think you are about to forget on the back of the test sheet— names, dates, definitions.

If you have not been keeping up with your class, it will be practically impossible for you to present and support an independent interpretation of something. All you may be capable of doing is a "data dump." It is better than nothing. Take all the facts and ideas you know and organize them into some sort of logical outline. Then write down every little thing you memorized, but do so without the framework of an organized narrative. Don't just transcribe your outline. If you can attempt an interpretation, do so. Keep your handwriting neat and free of glaring grammar and spelling errors.

Note to Self

Read the Instructions and Watch the Time

We stressed this over and over in chapter seven, but it is even more important when you are under serious pressure and feeling nervous. Always take the time to read the instructions carefully and make sure you don't get hung up too long on any one question. Budget your time wisely.

On Multiple-Choice and Short-Answer Tests. The triage method (described in detail in chapter seven) will stand you in good stead on both of these formats. As soon as you get your test paper, go through and answer every question you know flat out, skipping questions that you are unsure about. Your grasp of the material you just crammed won't last long, so get those answers down before you forget anything.

If you have a gut reaction about the answer to a question—like you just have the feeling that "Ulysses S. Grant" is the answer, but you aren't really sure you could explain why you feel that way—go with it and don't look back. Your first instinct is usually right. When you cram, your brain soaks up more information than you are aware of. That gut feeling may be some piece of buried knowledge trying to assert itself.

When you run across a multiple-choice question to which you don't know the answer, remember to use process of elimination to improve your chances of guessing correctly. See if you can identify the answer choices that are definitely wrong, cross them out, then make your best guess from the remaining options. Excluding even one answer choice tilts the odds in your favor.

The One-Day Paper-Writing Plan

If you have a major paper due in under two days, you've got big problems. But you already knew that. Prepare to remain chained to your desk until you are done, and cancel all other obligations. Here is the down-and-dirty, one-day paper-writing plan:

Step One: Pick a topic you have already mastered. Remember how in chapter nine we talked about adapting your paper topic to your interests? Well in this case, you need to adapt your paper topic to your strengths. If you can draw on past research or tilt the topic toward something you are very familiar with, do so. It will help if you have a few books on the subject. It is acceptable to do a paper on a topic you have covered before, provided you are bringing something new to the subject. It is not acceptable to turn in the exact same paper you wrote for another class. If you are lost, flip through your textbook and look for any mention of a controversy in the field you are studying. You might want to take sides and argue your point.

Step Two: Write an outline and figure out what kinds of information you will need. Feasibility is key. You will not have time to hunt down obscure information.

Step Three: If you have remote access to your library's filing system, do your subject searches from home and prepare a list of books and articles you want. Spend no more than one hour doing this. If you don't have remote access, combine step three with step four.

Step Four: Launch a commando raid on the library. Go in, gather your materials, and get out in under an hour.

Step Five: Skim through your sources and refine your topic based on feasibility. You don't have time to go back to the library and start again, but you can refocus your thesis to make the paper more interesting or easier to write.

Step Six: Rewrite your outline, leaving lots and lots of space between lines. You will be taking notes on this outline sheet.

Step Seven: Read through your sources. Whenever you find a piece of information you want to use, write it, along with the author's last name and the page number on which it appears, into your outline in the appropriate section. Your outline may get a little messy and crazy, but do your best to keep it organized.

Step Eight: Take a break for half an hour or so. Eat something, take a walk. Let the ideas you have just raced through settle into your brain.

Step Nine: Write your first draft and your bibliography. Don't worry about grammar or spelling. Just get your ideas hooked together.

Step Ten: Take another break for half an hour or so. Drink some juice. Take a shower. Do what you must to freshen up, but don't load up on coffee because you are almost done, and will soon want to sleep.

Step Eleven: Create your final draft. Read through your paper and touch it up as best you can, make sure you have satisfied your teacher's formatting requirements, run the spell checker on the document (if you are using a computer), and print or type a clean, neat copy.

Step Twelve: Put your paper in your book bag and go to sleep.

KAPLAN

DON'T GET DISCOURAGED

No matter how it happened, getting off track at school can be pretty unsettling. You might feel like a deer trapped in the headlights of an oncoming car, frightened and frozen and incapable of doing anything to save yourself from certain doom. You might even be tempted to give up because the effort involved in getting your academic life back together seems too great.

But you are not a deer, and you are not trapped. You can save yourself if you want to. You just have to decide that persevering is worthwhile and that doing well in school is worthwhile. You have to make up your mind not to be the kind of person who shrinks from anything that is difficult. You can do it.

To help you get through your moments of doubt and panic, in chapter 11 we have pulled together some quotes, facts, lyrics, pictures, jokes, and other odds and ends to inspire you, make you laugh, and help you to keep your chin up.

Section 4

Food for Your Brain

Chapter 11

A Month of Motivations

Is your passion for learning petering out? Is your spunk for study sputtering? Your yen for wisdom yawning? Did you just get a bad grade on your last test, throw up your hands and scream, "What's the use?" We all feel our motivation slip and our confidence dip from time to time. You have to learn how to put minor setbacks into perspective, pick yourself up, and get back in the saddle. To help you, we have gathered a variety of inspirational thoughts and advice from many different sources. Some are serious and touching, some are silly, and some are downright corny. We hope they help you get past the blahs and encourage you to keep swinging.

SOME HIGH-POWER SONGS

Ever hear of the Volga boatmen? They had to row big boats up and down the Volga river in Russia. On a scale of one to ten, that job rates a negative twelve. But they sang a song while they rowed, and maybe that kept them going. Take a tip from them and never, ever get a job rowing Russian boats. And find a song that is your personal motivational anthem. Here are some lines from a few songs you might want to listen to:

"I'm doin' all right, makin' good grades/The future's so bright I gotta wear shades."—Timbuk3. This is an '80s one-hit wonder band, but this song inspired countless Reagan-era teens to seek high-paying jobs.

"Mama may have/Papa may have/But God bless the child that's got his own."—"God Bless the Child," cowritten and most famously performed by blues legend Billie Holiday

"And what it all comes down to/Is that everything's gonna be fine, fine, fine."—Alanis Morrisette, "Hand In My Pocket"

"Trouble in mind, I'm blue/But I won't be blue always/'Cause the sun's gonna shine/In my back door some day."—"Trouble in Mind," blues standard by R. M. Jones

"There are problems in these times/But WOOOO! None of them are mine . . ."—"Beginning to See the Light" by The Velvet Underground (because sometimes it is nice to think of all the things that aren't your responsibility)

"Walk on through the wind/Walk on through the rain/Though your dreams be tossed and blown/Walk on, walk on, with hope in your heart/And you'll never walk alone/You'll never walk alone."—"You'll Never Walk Alone" from *Carousel* by Richard Rodgers and Oscar Hammerstein II

"We are the champions, my friend/And we'll keep on fighting till the end/We are the champions/We are the champions/No time for losers 'cause we are the champions."—"We Are the Champions," by Queen

WE LOVE WINSTON

When it comes to motivational speakers, it is hard to top Winston Churchill, Prime Minister of England during World War II. He managed to rally an entire country against terrifying odds.

"We are all worms, but I think I am a glow worm."—Winston Churchill. Some people think that Britain's valiant leader was drunk when he said this, but it is a nice sentiment, anyway.

> ### *Mind Boost*
>
> *Online Oomph*
>
> It the few quotes and ideas on these pages aren't enough, try browsing through the hundreds of inspirational thoughts online at:
>
> www.cyber-nation.com/victory/quotations

"A pessimist sees the difficulty in every opportunity; an optimist sees the opportunity in every difficulty."—Winston Churchill

VICTORY . . .

"Victory at all costs, victory in spite of all terror, victory however long and hard the road may be; for without victory there is no survival."—Winston Churchill, in a speech to the House of Commons, May 13, 1940

"We shall not flag or fail. We shall go on to the end. We shall fight in France, we shall fight on the seas and oceans, we shall fight with growing confidence and growing strength in the air, we shall defend our island, whatever the cost may be, we shall fight on the beaches, we shall fight on the landing grounds, we shall fight in the fields and in the streets, we shall fight in the hills; we shall never surrender."—Winston Churchill, addressing the House of Commons on June 4, 1940. His speeches really make you feel like a wimp for even considering giving up, don't they?

MISCELLANEOUS MUSINGS AND ADVICE

"People are just about as happy as they make up their minds to be."—Abraham Lincoln

"Experience is the name everyone gives to their mistakes."—Oscar Wilde, *Lady Windermere's Fan*. As long as you learn from them, all mistakes are worthwhile.

"Life can only be understood backwards, but lived forwards."—Søren Kierkegaard, a philosopher. Sadly, Kierkegaard's comments do not apply to calculus, but this may help you remember that when you feel lost, you are not alone.

"If you're going to be able to look back on something and laugh about it, you might as well laugh about it now."—Marie Osmond, squeaky-clean singer and entertainer known best for the '70s variety show she and her brother Donny hosted.

"As long as you're going to be thinking anyway, think big."—Donald Trump, real estate tycoon

"The best things in life aren't things."—Art Buchwald

"In three words I can sum up everything I've learned about life—it goes on."—Robert Frost

"Ah, but a man's reach should exceed his grasp—or what's a heaven for?"—Robert Browning

"Obstacles are those frightful things you see when you take your eyes off your goal."—Henry Ford

WAIT, WHERE AM I SUPPOSED TO BE LOOKING?

"Keep your eyes on the stars, and your feet on the ground."—Theodore Roosevelt, former president

"Keep your feet on the ground and keep reaching for the stars."—Casey Kasem, *American Top 40 Countdown*

"Keep your eyes on the road, your hands upon the wheel."—Jim Morrison, The Doors, "Roadhouse Blues"

ON COURAGE AND WINNING

"Courage is resistance to fear, mastery of fear—not absence of fear."—Mark Twain, *Pudd'nhead Wilson*

"Know your enemy and know yourself and you can fight 100 battles without defeat."—Sun Tzu, *The Art of War*

"Never let the fear of striking out get in your way."—George Herman "Babe" Ruth

"He only earns his freedom and his life who takes them every day by storm."—Johann Wolfgang von Goethe, *Faust*

"Great spirits have always encountered violent opposition from mediocre minds."—Albert Einstein

ON SELF-CONFIDENCE

"Show me someone not full of herself and I'll show you a hungry person."—Nikki Giovanni, poet, from "Poem for a Lady Whose Voice I Like"

"What the superior man seeks is in himself. What the mean man seeks is in others."—Confucius, ancient Chinese philosopher

"No one can make you feel inferior without your consent."—Eleanor Roosevelt, activist and wife of President Franklin D. Roosevelt, from *This Is My Story*

"If one advances confidently in the direction of his dreams, and endeavors to live the life which he has imagined, he will meet with a success unexpected in common hours."—Henry David Thoreau, American philosopher, *Walden*

"It's kind of fun to do the impossible."—Walt Disney

"Every calling is great when greatly pursued."—Oliver Wendell Holmes

"I am the greatest."—Muhammed Ali, former heavyweight boxing champion of the world. Luckily, you don't have to knock anyone out to believe in yourself.

MOVIES THAT WILL MOVE YOU

There is nothing like watching a feel-good movie with a triumphant hero to help pull you out of the dumps and inspire you to keep trying. You can think of a couple of examples of such movies yourself. Here are some we like:

The Bad News Bears (1976) starring Walter Matthau and Tatum O'Neal. This is a funny movie about a bunch of inept Little Leaguers whose coach helps them transform themselves into a great team. Great for a laugh and a reminder that with some hard work, anyone can succeed.

Braveheart (1995) starring Mel Gibson. Rousing story of Scottish hero William Wallace and his unlikely successes against the larger, superior British forces. It earned an Academy Award for Best Picture.

The Color Purple (1985) starring Whoopi Goldberg, Danny Glover, and Oprah Winfrey. Both warm and touching, this is the story of a rural Georgia woman's struggle for self-esteem and freedom. She is another odds-beater, and her hard-won triumphs make you feel so good.

The Corn Is Green (1945) starring Bette Davis. Yes, it is in black and white, and yes, it is old—but it is still good. Davis stars as a school teacher in a poor Welsh town who helps a student make it to Oxford University.

The Count of Monte Cristo (1934 or 1974). Both the old and the newer versions of this swashbuckling movie are great if you are in a mean mood and want to blame your recent setbacks on others for a while. This is a story of Edmond Dantes, a man wrongly imprisoned for murder, who spends his life seeking revenge against those who deliberately wronged him. Watch this, and maybe you can save yourself the trouble of hounding your enemies yourself. You can let Dantes work out your frustrations for you.

The Miracle Worker (1962) starring Anne Bancroft and Patty Duke. What could be more inspiring than the true story of Helen Keller, both blind and deaf, learning to understand the world around her and communicate with others? Get out your handkerchief.

My Brilliant Career (1979) starring Judy Davis. Set in turn-of-the-century Australia, this is the story of a young woman who defies everyone's expectations and fiercely pursues independence and knowledge.

My Left Foot (1989) starring Daniel Day-Lewis. True story of Christy Brown, a young man struck with cerebral palsy that leaves him able to use only his left leg. Despite the fact that everyone in the Irish town he is from thinks he is disabled mentally as well as physically, he teaches himself to write and paint. In fact, the movie is based on his autobiography.

Rocky (1976) starring Sylvester Stallone. Even the theme song from this movie has become synonymous with "inspirational." Stallone plays a no-name boxer who gets a shot at the title. If you have never seen it, check it out, even if you don't like boxing. It won several Academy Awards that year, including Best Picture.

What's Love Got to Do With It? (1993) starring Angela Bassett. True story of singer Tina Turner's struggle to free herself from an abusive marriage, and her rise to solo success. The music, if nothing else, will get you going.

When We Were Kings (1996) starring Muhammed Ali and George Foreman. A very cool documentary about an aging Muhammed Ali's 1974 heavyweight title fight in Zaire against the much younger, bigger George Foreman. The movie shows you just what kind of champion Ali was, and how brains, brawn, and willpower can always triumph over brawn alone.

Willy Wonka and the Chocolate Factory (1971) starring Gene Wilder. Something about those Oompa-loompas and that river of chocolate always cheers us up. It shows a young boy richly rewarded for sticking by his principles and doing what he knows is right.

Whatever You Do, Don't Give Up!

All the songs, movies, quotes, and other tidbits in chapter 11 can boost your mood when you are down or make you brave when you would rather hide under the bed and avoid school and the world in general for a while. But what works perfectly for us might leave you cold. It's important that you develop your own collection of morale props and your own confidence-building rituals to keep you pressing forward toward your goals. So if what makes you feel good is dancing around in your underwear and lip-synching "Disco Inferno" turned up full blast, by all means, do it. (Just lock your bedroom door to prevent embarrassing interruptions.)

As we said at the beginning of this book, developing good study habits isn't always easy. You may find yourself slipping into old, ineffective study habits from time to time. Don't give up and don't lose heart! If you consciously, consistently put into practice the advice in this book, you will see you grades climb. You will feel your confidence in your intelligence and your abilities growing. You will notice your parents and instructors taking a new interest in your work. And when that happens, you will discover that academic success feeds on itself. Your own sense of pride in your accomplishments will become your main motivation (although you

Keep Pressing Forward!

may still need "Disco Inferno" from time to time when the going gets rough). You might even find out that discovering new worlds of knowledge is fun and satisfying for its own sake. There is no need to take our word for it. Go out there and find out for yourself.

Good luck and good learning!

KAPLAN

Section 5

Reference

Web Resources

GENERAL REFERENCE

Dictionary.com
www.dictionary.com
Online dictionary, thesaurus, translator, word of the day, and more.

Internet Public Library
www.ipl.org/
Online reference collection plus access to more than 20,000 online books.

Bartleby.com: Great Books Online
www.bartleby.com
Combines the best of both classic and contemporary reference works into a comprehensive library.

Writing.com
www.writing.com
Online community for writers of all ages and levels of experience, packed with useful tips, resources, and networking opportunities.

America Online Research & Learn Web Center
www.aol.com/webcenters/research/home.adp
Links to a variety of helpful resources in various subjects.

Online Newspapers.com
www.onlinenewspapers.com
Directory of links to more than 10,000 newspapers around the world, searchable by country.

The Math Forum
mathforum.org
Online math resource for all grade levels, from elementary school through grad school.

U.S. Bureau of Labor Statistics
www.bls.gov
Source for useful statistics on jobs, salaries, education levels—great for beefing up a term paper (just be sure you cite where you found your material!).

SPECIAL CONSIDERATIONS

The Black Collegian Online
www.black-collegian.com
Career resources for African American students.

Association on Higher Education and Disability (AHEAD)
www.ahead.org
Organization has a job bank, training programs, and other valuable resources for students with disabilities.

Educational Testing Service Office of Disability Policy
www.ets.org/disability/index.html
Info on accommodations that can be arranged for paper-based and computer-based tests.

MISCELLANEOUS

Kaplan, Inc.
www.kaptest.com
Your one-stop destination on the Web for test prep, admissions, and success in school and careers.

U.S. Department of Education
www.ed.gov
Government site providing a wide range of info for students and educators, including some helpful sections on financial aid.

Amazon.com
www.amazon.com/books
Reliable online bookstore that lets you browse titles by category, then gives you a synopsis of each book, along with other recommendations, customer reviews, and more.

How Did We Do? Grade Us.

Thank you for choosing a Kaplan book. Your comments and suggestions are very useful to us. Please answer the following questions to assist us in our continued development of high-quality resources to meet your needs.

The title of the Kaplan book I read was: _____

My name is: _____

My address is: _____

_____

My e-mail address is:

What overall grade would you give this book?	Ⓐ Ⓑ Ⓒ Ⓓ Ⓕ
How relevant was the information to your goals?	Ⓐ Ⓑ Ⓒ Ⓓ Ⓕ
How comprehensive was the information in this book?	Ⓐ Ⓑ Ⓒ Ⓓ Ⓕ
How accurate was the information in this book?	Ⓐ Ⓑ Ⓒ Ⓓ Ⓕ
How easy was the book to use?	Ⓐ Ⓑ Ⓒ Ⓓ Ⓕ
How appealing was the book's design?	Ⓐ Ⓑ Ⓒ Ⓓ Ⓕ

What were the book's strong points? _____

How could this book be improved? _____

Is there anything that we left out that you wanted to know more about?

Would you recommend this book to others?   ☐ YES   ☐ NO

Other comments: _____

_____

_____

Do we have permission to quote you?   ☐ YES   ☐ NO

Thank you for your help.
Please tear out this page and mail it to:

>   Content Manager
>   Kaplan Test Prep & Admissions
>   1440 Broadway, 8th floor
>   New York, NY 10018

KAPLAN

Thanks!

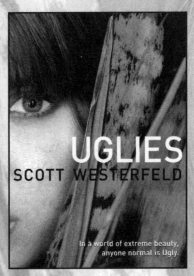
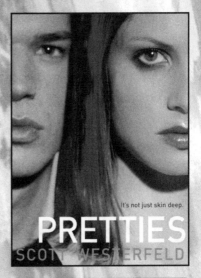